First World War
and Army of Occupation
War Diary
France, Belgium and Germany

46 DIVISION
Divisional Troops
233 Brigade Royal Field Artillery
1 February 1915 - 29 August 1916

WO95/2674/3

The Naval & Military Press Ltd
www.nmarchive.com
Published in association with The National Archives

Published by

The Naval & Military Press Ltd

Unit 10 Ridgewood Industrial Park,

Uckfield, East Sussex,

TN22 5QE England

Tel: +44 (0) 1825 749494

www.naval-military-press.com

www.nmarchive.com

This diary has been reprinted in facsimile from the original. Any imperfections are inevitably reproduced and the quality may fall short of modern type and cartographic standards.

© Crown Copyright
Images reproduced by permission of The National Archives, London, England, 2015.

Contents

Document type	Place/Title	Date From	Date To
Heading	WO95/2674/3 233 Brigade Royal Field Artillery (includes Separate Diaries By 2nd Derby Battery)		
Heading	46th Division Divl Artillery 4th Nth Mid'd (Became:- 233rd Brigade R.F.A. Feb 1915 Aug 1916 Bde Broken Up		
Heading	WO95/2674/2 (2nd Derby Battery) 233 Brigade R.F.A. 27/2/15 To 31/7/15		
Heading	North Midland Division. 2nd Derbys. Batty RFA (1/4 N.M. Hord Bde RFA) Vol I 27.2-30.4.15		
War Diary	S'hampton	27/02/1915	27/02/1915
War Diary	S'hampton Water	28/02/1915	28/02/1915
Heading	Le Havre	01/03/1915	02/03/1915
War Diary	In The Train	03/03/1915	03/03/1915
War Diary	Steenwerke	04/03/1915	04/03/1915
War Diary	Le Grand Munque	04/03/1915	06/04/1915
War Diary	Zwynebak	07/04/1915	30/04/1915
Heading	46th Division. 2nd Derby Batty (4th NM Howr Bde) RFA Vol II 1-31.5.15		
War Diary		01/05/1915	31/05/1915
Heading	46th Division 2nd Derbyshire Batty. (1/4 NM Bde.) RFA Vol III 1-6-31-29-15		
War Diary		01/06/1915	31/07/1915
Heading	North Midland Division 4th NM (Howzr) Bde. RFA (T) Vol I 1-28.2.15. Embarked Southampton 28.2.15		
War Diary	B-Stortford	01/02/1915	28/02/1915
Heading	North Midland Division. 1/4th N.M. Howzr Bde. RFA. Vol II 1-31.3.15 Embarked Havre 1.3.15 Bde Ht Petit Pont & Ploegsteert		
War Diary		01/03/1915	31/03/1915
Heading	North Midland Division. 4th N.M. (Howz) Bde RFA Vol III 1-30.4.15		
Heading	1/4 North Midland Howitzer 3rd Brigade R.F.A. 'T' War Diary From April 1st 1915 To April 30th 1915		
War Diary		01/04/1915	30/04/1915
Heading	46th Division 1/4 N M (Howz) Bde RFA. Vol IV 1-31.5.15		
War Diary		01/05/1915	31/05/1915
Heading	46th Division. 1/4 N.M. Bde R.F.A. Vol VI 1-31.8.15		
War Diary		01/08/1915	31/08/1915
Heading	46th Division. 1/4th N.M. (Howitzer) Bde RFA Vol V 1-30.6.15		
War Diary	Dranoutre	01/06/1915	24/06/1915
War Diary	Boeschepe	25/06/1915	30/06/1915
Heading	War Diary Of 1/4th North Midland (Howitzer) Bde. R.F.A. From 1.6.15 To 30.6.15		
Heading	46th Division. 1/4 N.M. Bde R.F.A. Vol VI 1-31-7-15		
War Diary	Boeschepe & Ypres	01/07/1915	03/07/1915
War Diary	Ypres	04/07/1915	31/07/1915
Heading	46th Division. 1/4th N.M. Bde R.F.A. Vol VIII Sept. 15		
War Diary	Ypres	01/09/1915	30/09/1915

Heading	46th Division. 1/4th N.M. Bde R.F.A. Oct 1915 Vol IX		
War Diary	Ypres Vieux Berquin Lillers	01/10/1915	04/10/1915
War Diary	Lillers & Labeuvriere	05/10/1915	11/10/1915
War Diary	Vermelles	11/10/1915	22/10/1915
War Diary	Vermelles & Labeuvriere	22/10/1915	25/10/1915
War Diary	Labeuvriere	26/10/1915	31/10/1915
Heading	46th Division. 1/4th N.M. Bde. R.F.A. Nov. Vol X		
Heading	War Diary Of 1/4th North Midland (Howitzer) Bde. R.F.A. From 1st-30th November 1915		
War Diary	Labeuvriere	01/11/1915	30/11/1915
War Diary		25/11/1915	27/11/1915
Heading	War Diary 1/4th: North Midland Brigade. R.F.A. 46 December 1st: to 31st: 1915. Vol XI		
War Diary		01/12/1915	16/12/1915
War Diary	In The Field	17/12/1915	31/12/1915
Heading	1/4 N.M. Bde R.F.A. Jan 1916 Vol XII		
War Diary	In The Field	01/01/1916	31/01/1916
Heading	War Diary. 4th. North Midland Brigade. R.F.A. February 1st:- 29th: 1916 Vol XIII		
Heading	1/4th North Midland (Howitzer) Brigade RFA War Diary from 1st February 1916 to 29th February 1916		
War Diary	In The Field	01/02/1916	29/02/1916
Heading	War Diary. 4th. North Midland Brigade. R.F.A. March 1st to 31st: 1916 Vol XIV		
Heading	1/4th North Mid. (Hour) Brigade R.F.A. War Diary. for March 1916		
War Diary	In The Field	01/03/1916	31/03/1916
Heading	1/4th North Midland (Howitzer) Brigade. R.F.A. 'T' War Diary. from 1st to 30th April 16 Vol XV		
War Diary	In The Field	01/04/1916	30/04/1916
Heading	War Diary. 23rd. Brigade. R.F.A. Late 1/4 N M Bde May 1st: to 31st: 1916 Vol 16		
Heading	233rd Brigade R.F.A. War Diary for the Month of May 1916		
War Diary	In The Field	01/05/1916	31/05/1916
Heading	War Diary. Headquarters 23rd Brigade. R.F.A. June 1st: to June 30th: 1916 Vol 17		
Heading	War Diary of 23rd Brigade, R.F.A. June 1916		
War Diary	In The Field	01/06/1916	30/06/1916
Heading	War Diary. 233rd: Brigade. R.F.A. July 1st: to July 31st: 1916 Vol 18		
War Diary	In The Field	01/07/1916	31/07/1916
Heading	War Diary. 233rd: Brigade. R.F.A. August 1st: to August 31st: 1916. Vol 19		
War Diary	In The Field	01/08/1916	29/08/1916
Miscellaneous	Re-organization of Divisional Artillery.	28/08/1916	28/08/1916

wo/95/2674/3

233 Brigade Royal Field Artillery

(include seperate diaries by
2nd Derry Battery)

46TH DIVISION
DIVL ARTILLERY

4TH NTH MID'D (BECAME :-
233RD BRIGADE R.F.A.
FEB 1915 AUG 1916.

Bde Broken Up

WO 95/2674/2

(2nd De Roy Battery) 233 Brigade R.F.A.
27/2/12 to 31/7/15

121/5/94

North Midland Division

2nd Clarkes: Betty RFA
(1/u N.M. Hos² B²e RFA)

Vol I 27.2 — 30.4.15

Hour date & Place	Summary of events & information	Remarks Ref & Appendices
Feb. 27 1915 S'hampton	Embarked on S.S "Tintoretto" at about 11. a.m - All guns & waggons & all horses (128) 1 Officer (Lt. Haslam) & 30 N.C.O's & men left at Rest Camp. 3 officers & 110 N.C.O's & men on board. Left Dock (Berth 46) about 4.30 P.M & moved out into Southampton Water. Anchored off Netley	
Feb. 28 in S'hampton Water	At anchor all day. Horses & men quite comfortable & plenty of forage & food. Sailed at 8.30 P.M under escort of 2 Torpedo boats & crossed Channel	17

Hour date & place	Summary of events & information	Reference Remarks & Appendices
Mar. 1 Le Havre	Reached Le Havre early morning & came into Dock about 10. a.m. Off-loaded men & horses & their vehicles. Drew Stores, (Coats warm British, Boots etc etc) from Ordnance Stores. Left the Docks 5 pm & marched to No 2 Camp. Guns & horses in the open Officers & men under Canvas.	
Mar. 2 Le Havre	Exercise order & "Cleaning up" in the morning. Left Camp 5.30 pm & marched to Station for entrainment (Gare de marchandise Point 1). Loaded Horses (8 per truck) & Guns & Vehicles - also forage & rations for 2 days. Left Le Havre 10.39 P.M.	

Hour date & place	Summary of events & information	Remarks Ref & Appendices
Mar.3 on the train STEENWERCK	Travelled via Rouen, Callais, Abbeville & Hazebruck to Steenwercke arriving at 7 P.M. Off loaded men & horses – fatigue party to unload vehicles – Marched to MENEGATE Farm (about 3 miles) Guns & horses in the open, Officers & men in Billets. Vet.y Lt. Newton attached to Bty.	
Mar 4 Le Grand Munque	Bty. H.Q. Gns & R.t X moved to Le Grand Munque Farm near PETIT PONT – L.t X (under Capt. MacMichael) to Le Bizet to be attached to XIV Bgde R.F.A. R.t X guns placed in prepared positions near road leading from PETIT PONT to Armentiers – Horses of both sec.ns	

Hour date & place	Summary of events & information	Remarks Ref & Appendices
	sent back to MENEGATE with all Drivers.	
Mar. 5 Le Grand Munque	Fired 20 rounds in the morning observing from CHATEAU LA HUTTE at TILLEUL FARM & registered range to same. Fired 20 rounds in the afternoon at farm in U 16 c South & registered range to same. 1 Officer (Lt Haslam) & 30 N.C.Os & men rejoined this evening.	
Mar 6	Unable to fire observing from ST IVES owing to faulty telephone wire — fired 6 rounds in afternoon	

Place, Date & Hour		Remarks Reference & Appendices
Mar. 7. LaGrand Munque	Observing from CHATEAU LA HUTTE – but unable to register. 2/Lt W.E.Balcombe Brown came (attached) from 4th Div. Am. Col. Observation Stn. ST IVES Night Line of No 3 Gun U 16 C West on road registered. 21 rounds fired 19 " handed over to 1st Bty. for Bombardment of Enemy trench	
Mar. 8 do.	Obs. Statn. ST IVES 8 rounds fired to register No 2 Night Lines. U 22 a W on road. 8 rounds fired on breastwork U 16. C West	
Mar 9 00	Obs. Statn. LE GHEER 4 rounds fired to check night lines 12 " " at ruin U 22 C 77.	

21

Mar. 10 Le Grand Munque	Obsn Station LE GHEER 16 rounds fired (at 4.30 P.M) to bombard 2 farms U 16 c & d South — range obtained & several hits in enemy trenches.
Mar 11 Do	Obsn Stn LE GHEER — also from ST IVES 16 rounds fired (at 1 P.M) to flatten out ruined farm at U 16. c. West. Observation v. difficult owing to mist & bad light — also owing to telephone wire from ST IVES being cut by Shrapnel — (Lt DANBY 13513th wounded head & arm) not many effectives. Moved to Veuve Louis Dutilleul Farm (¼ mile)

22

Mar. 12. Obs: Le Gheer Tgt. Farm Houses
U 16 d S.W. 8 rounds in morning 12.37 PM
range registered 4175 yds. No 2 & 3 Gun
afternoon. Tgt. House behind barricade
U 22 C 5.6. Fairly successful — 1st gun
erratic (No 2)   Total 16 rnds

Mar 13   Obs: (morning) St/IVES. Tgt. Ruined Bldg
U 16 C W.. (11 rounds) v. Successful series
Obs. St. heavily shelled & "look-out" demolished
Obs (aftn) Le Gheer Tgt. Bird Cage
U 26 b E to U 22 a W — 5 rnds Effective
Work on new gun posn begun, 1800x forward of Total 16 rnds
                                 present posn

Mar 14 Obs: Au Gheer Staminet (morning)
Tgt. U 22 d S.W Loophole Farm. a v.
successful series — (10 rounds) No 2 Gun
Obs: Le Gheer (au Commerce) aftn Tgt. U16d
S.W. No 3 gun 6 rounds — Effect fair
  Paid Rd X Gunners.

Mar. 15 Obs⁻ Le GHEER. Tgt Farm U 16 d.s.w
Farm Bldgs. 10 rounds. Fairly effective
N R B E took series. (C.O. came up to
watch)
also (aft⁻) Tgt "Birdcage" 6 rounds
(N R B E) one direct hit & fair effect.

Mar. 16. Weather v. dull & misty. did not
open fire. Work on new pos⁻
progressing well.

Mar. 17. Obs⁻ Le Gheer. No rounds fired.
Nothing particular doing.

Mar. 18. Situation normal. No rounds fired
Work on new position. (Q.M.S. to Waggon Lines)

Mar. 19. Situation normal. No firing. V. cold
snow showers all day. Working party
on new gun position.

Mar 20.	Situation normal. No rounds fired. Working party on new gun position. remainder Musketry, Stretcher Drill etc.
Mar 21	as above
Mar 22	as above
Mar 23	as above men to PONT de NIEPPE for Bathing
Mar 24	as March 20th
Mar 25	as March 23rd
Mar 26	Fired 2 rounds - (1 from each gun) to empty guns for cleaning -

Mar 27	Situation normal. No rounds fired. Sir H Smith-Dorrien came round in afts & looked at guns & detachments. 2/Lt Balcombe Brown left (to go to 14th F.A.B)
Mar 28	as March 25th. Lt H E Whaley attached for duty
Mar 29 — 30 — 31	as March 28th.
April 1 — 2	as above.
" 3	as above. Lt Joyce joined for duty from 2/4th N.M. Byde
" 4	Situation normal. B.C reported to G.O.C RA Vth Divn at 9am re^ed occupation of new posn & inspected same & selected posn with Col Strong (O.C. XV F.A.B) Lt Whaley retd to Hd Qrs.

26

Ap. 5 — Situation normal. No rounds fired. B.C at new posⁿ selecting billets etc & going round Obsⁿ stations.

Ap. 6 — Situation normal. Battery moved to new posⁿ at Zwynebak (1¼ miles N. of NEUVE EGLISE) T 36. 6.7. RX guns under B.C. LX guns under Capt MacMichael. LX Waggons under Lt. Haslam. RX Waggon & 1 X Amⁿ Colⁿ (attached) under Lt. Eddowes.
RX guns in position by 8 p.m. Remainder got blocked by 1st N.M. Bde R.F.A coming into new position & did not get in till 10.30 p.m. Waggons & horses out practically all night.

Zwynebak
Ap. 7 — Situation normal. Gunners in billet 100ˣ from guns – also 3 Officers – Drivers & Waggon line at small farm about ¾ mile in rear. Remaining officers (2) at small farm between the above.
Work in posⁿ – completing gun platforms
Bᵗ attached to 1st N.M Bde R.F.A (Col Fonge) etc

N.B
Working party under 2t Joyce at work on new gun posⁿ all day – preparing same.

27

Ap. 8	Situation normal. Work on gun position continued & 2 new emplacements for LX completed - also dug out for telephone. 8 rounds fired in aftⁿ Obsⁿ from The Convent. NEUVE-EGLISE with No 1 gun - to register line
Ap. 9	Situation normal. Fired 12 rounds in morning to register IV. Lines for LX. Obsⁿ from dug-out T.18 b. 9. 8. (on forward slope of "63") Fired 4 rounds in aftⁿ. Obsⁿ from The Convent with No 2 gun to register line. Zone allotted to Batt^y pointed out to all officers
Ap 10.	Situation normal. Fired 12 rnds in aftⁿ Obsⁿ from WULVERGHEM HOUSE - to register Farm N.36 d. Changed W.L to new position vacated by 130 Bt^y
Ap. 11.	Fired 9 rnds. Obsⁿ from KEMMEL - not v. satisfact^y obsⁿ as so far back
Ap. 12	Situation normal. Inspected alternative posⁿ (in rear) Re-attached to own Brigade. Fired 10 rnds in aftⁿ obs from Wulverghem. 5 hits good series

Ap. 13	Situation unchanged. Fired 1 round by order of G.O.C. N. Mid: Div— (to test communication)
Ap. 14	No rounds fired - Situation unchanged
Ap. 15	Situation normal. Fired 19 rnds in aftn. Obsg from 115 Bd Obs: Stn ("63") to register X roads N.E. of KRUISSTRAAT X Rds not a very successful series. Obsn v. difficult. Order recd 11 p.m. to harness up Waggon Teams & all men to sleep in their boots.
Ap. 16.	Situation unchanged - No rounds fired
Ap. 17	Situation unchanged - No rounds fired. Working party started to prepare new gun position (in rear) T. 8 c S.E. A good posn behind hedge & well in rear of crest Platform rather wet & ground /water-logged Good road leading up to post.

April 18	Situation unchanged. No rounds fired. Work on new gun position
April 19.	Situation unchanged. Fired 12 rnds Obs? from WULVERGHEM. at trenches in N. 36 d. (R × guns) Working party on new gun position
April 20.	Situation normal. Fired 19 rnds Obs? from FRENCHMANS F^m at SPANBROEK MOLEN & trenches near same. (L × guns) Fairly Successful. Working party as above
April 21	Situation normal. No rounds fired Work on new position nearing completion
April 22	Situation unchanged. No rounds fired Working party on rear gun position.
~~April~~	Lindenhoek Cottage (Obsⁿ Stⁿ) Shelled about 4 P.M. to 6 P.M. by enemy high Explosive shells – about 30 in number.
April 23.	Situation normal. Fired 8 rounds (N°1 gun) at Farm U 1 a. Catchy wind – not v. successful series. Obs 25 N.C.O.s & men to Bath at BAILLEUL 10 A.Truck

April 24	Situation unchanged. Fired 10 rnds (all 4 guns) at Trenches round SPANBROEK MOLEN — obs? from FRENCHMAN'S F'm —
25 (Sunday)	Situation normal. Parties to R.C. & Wes'n Ch. Parades — also to work on rear pos'n. Fired 4 rounds (L X guns) at 8 pm on SPANBROEK MOLEN Trenches — retaliation effect fair.
26	Situation unchanged. No rounds fired. Working party as usual.
27	as above
28	Situation normal. 8 rounds fired at "fort" in rear of SPANBROEK MOLEN. (Forward obs. off'r on F 5 Trench) successful series. Working party as usual. Corrugated iron Sheets (36) and Sand Bags (400) rec'd

April 29	Situation normal. Fired 4 rnds at "Fot" in rear of SPANBROEK MOLEN. No working party. 25 N.C. O's & men to Baths at BAILLEUL
April 30	Situation unchanged. Fired 5 rnds as above. Obs. from G.2 & F.6 Trenches (by Inf'y Officers) not v. successful. Party of 20 N.C. O's & men to Baths at BAILLEUL

———— " ————

121/5354

A
86

46th Division

2nd Ser by Batty (4" NM Hrs' Bde) R+R.

Jortt 1 — 31.5.15.

May 1st	Situation normal. Fired 10 rnds in morning (11.am) at "fort" in rear of SPANBROEK MOLEN and 6 rnds at 6 pm at SPANBROEK MOLEN itself. Obs. in morning from F 5 trench — in aftn. from The Convent - N. EGLISE. Working party on new gun posn. making overhead cover to dug-outs with corrugated iron sheets.
May 2 (Sunday)	Situation unchanged - no rounds fired
May 3	Situation normal. 8 rnds fired at 6 pm at SPANBROEK MOLEN — retaliation
May 4	Situation unchanged. 8 rnds fired at 11.am at a fort located opposite No. 12 trench 8th round target.
May 5	Situation normal. Fired 8 rnds at same target as 4th May.
May 6	Situation unchanged. Working party on new posn. Bathing party (25 N.C.O's & men) to Bailleul. Fired 6 rnds at Farm 32 C. Capt Archdale came —

May 7.	Situation normal. Major Webber left & Capt Archdale took over as Adj't. Fired 12 rnds at Farm U1a. Obs'n from 10a.Trench (Lt Haslam) a good series & effective. Fired 2 rnds in aft'n at Spanbrock Molen trenches. Enemy fired H.E. explosive shell & small shrapnel over Lincoln Horse lines & 2nd Lines 73 Bty. Also 8 shell into field in which our new Gun pos'n is being prepared. No damage done. 2/Lt Eddowes att'd H'Qrs as O.O. Lt G.D. Wilson attached for duty from Am'n Col'n
May 8	Situation unchanged. No rounds fired
May 9 (Sunday)	Situation unchanged. 12 rounds fired at Fort opposite No 12 trench – Obs'n Off'r in No 12 trench. 6 rounds fired (7.25 P.M.) at SPANBROEK MOLEN Trenches (by order)
May 10	Situation normal. Fired 15 rnds (5.59 pm) to register tgts with Aeroplane obs'n. Result v. satisfactory – Time (5 tgts) 24 min.

34

May 11.	Situation normal. Working party on new Gun position as usual. Fired 5 rnds (at 8.34 pm.) by order of C.R.A at ~~French~~ Mortar on ~~road~~ WULVERGHEM-WAETCHAETE road (just short of KRUISSTRAATE X Rds) to silence Mortar
May 12	Situation unchanged. No rounds fired
May 13	Situation normal. Fired 10 rounds at Sap opposite E² trench (at request of Infantry) v. successful - 4 hits. Obsⁿ from E² Trench.
May 14	Situation unchanged. Fired 10 rounds at "Fort" opposite N° 12 Trench. successful series obsᵈ from N° 12 Trench. Lt Stowes returned from Hᵈ Qrs Lt Wilson rejoined Amⁿ Colⁿ
May 15	Situation normal - no rounds fired
May. 16 Sunday	Situation unchanged. Fired 5 rnds (in morning) at N.36 d & 9 in aftⁿ at fort in rear of Spts Molen

May 17.	Situation normal. Fired 6 rnds at Fort op.n No 12 Trench - with good Effect.
May 18.	Situation unchanged. Fired 10 rnds at same target as above - Effect fair. Work on new gun pos.n finished. Weather wet.
May 19	Situation normal. Weather still wet & dull. No rounds fired. 2 S.N.C.Os & men to Baths at BAILLEUL
May 20	Situation unchanged. Fired 10 rnds in morning at Fort op. No 12 Trench. Fair Effect. & 10 rnds at Sap op.te E2 Trench with fair results. E1 Right trench mined about 3.30 p.m
May 21.	Situation normal. 1 round only fired.
May 22	Situation unchanged. 5 rounds fired
May 23 (Sunday)	Situation normal. Fired 8 rnds before 12 (noon) at Sap. op.te E2 Trench. & 6 rnds later.
May 24	Situation unchanged. 11 rounds fired.

May 25.	Situation unchanged. Fired 5 rounds
May 26	Situation normal. Fired 14 rounds. 25 N.C.O's & men to Baths at Bailleul.
May 27	Situation unchanged. Fired 10. rnds
May 28	Situation normal. only 2 rnds fired
May 29	Situation unchanged. 3 rnds fired
May 30 (Sunday)	Situation normal. 4 rnds fired. Church parades for R.Cs & C. of E.
May 31	Situation unchanged. Fired 4 rounds

121/6306

46th Division

2nd Derbyshire Bathy: (1/4 NM Bde.) R+H.

Vol III

1-6-21-4-15

Mr

Date etc.	Summary of Events	Remarks
June 1.	Situation normal. Fired a Salvo at Sap opposite E2 Trench – effect fair.	
June 2.	Situation unchanged – fired 4 rnds (No 3 gun) at odd times during the day at same tgt. Obtained 1 direct hit	
June 3.	Situation normal. Fired 6 rnds at same tgt.	
June 4.	Situation unchanged. No rounds fired. 2/Lt Dufton attached from A[mm]n Col[um]n & 2/Lt Eddowes went to H.Qrs as Orderly Offr	
June 5.	Situation normal. Fired 14 rnds at Spanbroek Molen – by request of Infy – with good effect. Observed from Kemmel Hill.	
June 6. (Sunday)	Situation unchanged – No rnds fired – (Pay Day.)	
June 7.	Situation normal. Fired 6 rnds at Sap opp E2 Trench & 5 at Farm U1a. at request of Infy. Result satisfactory.	

Date	Summary of Events	Remarks
June 8	Situation unchanged. Fired 2 rnds at N.36.d.	
June 9	Situation normal. No rounds fired. Reconnoitred new gun position (for retirement to GHQ line) at S.12.b.9.5.	
June 10	Situation unchanged. No rnd fired	
June 11	Situation normal - Fired 18 rnds	
June 12	Situation unchanged - 6 rnd fired. Work on new (GHQ line) posⁿ begun.	
June 13 (Sunday)	Situation normal. No rnds fired. Ch. Pole. at Wagon Lines 2ⁿᵈ Lincolns.	
June 14	Situation unchanged - 8 rnds fired	
June 15	Situation normal. 4 rnds fired - J3 Trench blown up by enemy. Some casualties -	
June 16	"Situation unchanged. 50ᵗʰ Divⁿ ordered to advance & Infy to assault trenches at 4.10 a.m. 46ᵗʰ Divⁿ to "demonstrate" from 3 - 5 a.m. BC: at Ob. Stn. at 2.45 a.m. A dull misty morning - obsⁿ difficult - v. little activity on	

Date	Summary of Events	Remarks
	our front - only 7 rnds fired before 6 a.m. 4 during the morning, and 9 later in the day.	
June 17.	Situation normal. 12 rnds fired at Spanbroek Molen - by request of Infy - unsatisfactory results.	
June 18.	Situation unchanged. 9 rnds fired - Work on G.H.Q. posn finished.	
June 19.	Situation normal. 8 rnds fired.	
June 20 (Sunday)	Situation unchanged. No rounds fired - Enemy planes up early signalling over heavy batty. 1 H.E. shell dropped about 2.30 p.m close to old 130 Bty posn	
June 21	Situation normal. Fired 4 rounds - Adjt Northumbrian Brigade (5 incl) R.F.A came to look round posn	
June 22	Situation unchanged. No rounds fired - O.C 4th Durham (How) Bty came to look at posn & was shown Obsn Statn, etc etc.	

40

Date	Summary of Events	Remarks
June 23	Fired 2 rounds (to empty guns) & LX moved at night to new position near ABEELE. One X of Northumbrian Divn took over LX gun pits. Situation unchanged.	
June 24	Situation normal. Fired 2 rounds (to empty guns) Rt X. moved at night to new position – with Bgd Hd Qrs & 1st Battery.	
June 25	Arr'd new Position (near ABEELE) 2.30 a.m. Guns parked & Horse lines put out in large field with 1st Battery. Situation normal.	
June 26	Situation unchanged. Capt Macmichael & the C.O. having reconnoitred new position (I 15 a.2.3) the W.L. moved at 7.a.m. to H.21.b.7.5 & in the evening (8 PM) the gunners marched on to gun position as above.	
June 27 (Sunday)	Situation normal – Work on preparation of gun position. Bdr Gurr wounded by Schrapnel in arm & shoulder.	
June 28	Situation unchanged – Work on new position.	

42

Date	Summary of Events	Remarks
29 June	Situation unchanged. Work on position continued. Guns brought up from WL at 8.30pm and 9.50pm.	
30 June	Situation normal. Work on gun positions (under a good fence with row of trees a few yards from it & good cover) continued. Batt. attached to 49th Bgde R.F.A. 14th Divn. for duty.	

Date	Summary of Events	Remarks
July 1st	Situation normal. Fired 8 rnds in aft⁰ at trenches in front of Rly WOOD. At 5.25 P.M. one of our shells fell short (out of A.Sd gun) & dropped in the trench where Capt Mackintosh was observing, wounding him & Pte Sampton severely & killing Bdr Orme. The 2 former taken to Dressing St⁰ & then to Hospital, the latter buried behind N⁰ 10 trench.	
July 2nd	Situation unchanged. Lt Joyce came up from W.L. Fired 10 rounds in aft⁰ at Strong Point T 12 a.3.7. Not very satisfactory.	
July 3rd	Situation normal. No rounds fired. Work on gun position completed & dug-out made	
July 4th	Situation unchanged. Fired 20 rounds at W. Edge of DEADMAN'S BOTTOM. etc. Quite satisfactory	

Date	Summary of Events	Remarks
July 5.	Situation normal – Returned to 46th Divn & came under orders of O.C. 4th Bgde again. Fired 6 rounds (to register) on Triangle ~~Wood~~ Copse J.19.c.2.2.	
July 6	Situation unchanged – Fired 20 rounds at 6.45 (demonstration) during bombardment. and a further 7 rounds later at enemy gun at J.19.c.10.9	
July 7	Situation normal – no rounds fired	
" 8	do do	Lt Eddowes to W. Line
July 9	– " – Fired 24 rounds.	
" 10	– " – no rounds fired.	
July 11 (Sunday)	Situation unchanged – Fired 7 rounds	
July 12	⎱ Situation normal – no rounds fired.	
" 13	⎰ Detachments at work preparing new position.	
" 14	– " – Moved 3 guns into new position at I.27.a.7.8. (One gun to O.O. for repair) A very dark very wet night	

45

Date	Summary of Events	Remarks
	but all guns successfully moved into pos"	
July 15.	Situation normal. Fired 14 rounds – obs? from 36 Trench to register Nos. 2 & 3 guns.	
" 16.	Situation unchanged. Fired 14 rounds for further registration. Capt. H Lewis att⁴ for duty.	
" 17.	Situation normal. Fired 11 rounds with N° 4 Gun. N.B. This gun was unable to be fired before owing to water in gun pit.	
July 18 (Sunday)	Situation unchanged. 19 rounds fired. N° 3 Gun out of action to go to O.O for repair.	
July 19	Situation normal. 20 rounds fired (14 at "Hill 60" at 7.p.m) N.B. N° 1 Gun pit completed & gun registered on Hill 60.	
" 20	Situation unchanged. 16 rounds fired. Enemy Gun target J.25.C.2.1 registered – obs⁴ by F.O.O Staffs Bgde.	
" 21	Situation normal. Fired 10 rounds.	
" 22	———"——— " 12 " at a Gas Cylinder (?) on Hill 60.	

Date	Summary of Events	Remarks
July 23.	Situation normal. No rounds fired.	
" 24	—"— Fired 9 rnds at 1.35 A.M at request of Infy on Hill 60. and 12 in aftn	
July 25 (Sunday)	Situation unchanged. Ch. Parade (at 6th Staff'd Gun Posn) in morning. Fired 3 rnds (Obsd by Aeroplane) in Evening. Wireless outfit & operator attached to Bty. from No 6 Squadn RFC	
July 26	Situation normal. Fired 10 rnds in morning & 13 in aftn. The latter with A. Obs. v. satisfactory. Capt. Laws left Bty to go to Div. Am: Col. 30 N.C.O's & men to Baths at Poperinghe	
July 27.	Situation unchanged. 24 rnds fired. 14 with A.O. the latter v. successful.	
" 28	Situation normal — No rounds fired.	
" 29	—"— . Considerable activity in HOOGE area. Our Infy attacked, supported by Arty fire.	
" 30.	Situation about the same — Heavy bombardment by the enemy of HOOGE and district followed	

47

Date	Summary of Events	Remarks

by an Infy Attack which was preceeded by
"liquid fire". Our Infy driven out & about
500 yds of trenches lost. Fired 20 rounds
(at Hill 60) at 4 a.m – demonstration.
Attack by our Infy at 2.45 p.m – some lost
ground regained. Heavy Arty fire all
day. Fired 10 rounds (off the map) in aft⁰ at
an enemy Gun Tgt.

July 31. Situation unchanged. Heavy firing practically
all day. Called on by Infy at 3.6 am – but
only fired 2 rounds. Fired 8 rounds in aft⁰ obs⁰
by F.O.O. Staffs Bgde & Lt Cattle (1st D. Bty) and
20 rounds (on Hill 60) in Evening (6.30 pm) co-operating
with Infy Trench Mortar Bombardment. Result
satisfactory. V. heavy firing all evening till
about 10.30 p.m. with more fighting round HOOGE

a2

North Midland Division

121/4538

4th NM (Hows´r) Bde. R.F.A (T)

Vol I. 1-28.2.15

Embarked SOUTHAMPTON 28.2.15

DATE	PLACE	SUMMARY OF EVENTS AND INFORMATION	REMARKS REFERENCE APPENDICES
		C. 2118	
February 1.	B-STORTFORD	Training programme carried out. 1 Rider died 29.1.15.	
— 2		do. do.	
— 3.		do. do. Major Henry Lowe returned fr. SALISBURY.	
— 4		do. do.	
— 5		do. do.	
— 6		do. do. Lt Cattle returned fr. ALDERSHOT.	
— 7		Sunday.	
— 8.		Training Programme carried out (scheme set by CRA.) Major Crompton proceeded to be attached to B. Ex. Force. 3 cobs sent to ESSEX Yeomanry	
— 9.		Training programme carried out. Col. holds conference of Unit Commanders 6 p.m.	
— 10		do. do. C.R.A. holds conference of Bde. Comdrs. at Wharf Ho at 6. p.m.	
— 11		do. do. 9 cobs sent to A.S.C. Reserve Train N.M.D LUTON.	
— 12.		do. do. I.O.M. inspected guns. S.O.C. HMM. D. in. lectured on his experiences at the front. 1. L. D. received fr. mob. bt. See.	
— 13.		Training Programme carried out. 1 Rider died.	

DATE	SUMMARY OF EVENTS AND INFORMATION C.2118	REMARKS REFERENCE APPENDICES
14.2.15	Sunday. 1 L.H. Horse Died.	
15.2.15.	Training Programme carried out.	
16.2.15.	do. do. 3 water carts drawn.	
17.2.15.	do. do. 9 Canadian Cobs received.	
18.2.15.	do. do. 20 men joined f. 2/4 N.M. How. Bde.	
19.2.15.	Inspection of N.M. Div. at GREAT HALLINGBURY PARK by H.M. The King.	
20.2.15.	Training Programme carried out. 3 Chargers received. 1 Officer & 5 men f. 2/4 N.M. Brig	To take over stores.
21.2.15.	Sunday. 29 Horses received (6 Riders 13 L.h. 10 H.h.)	
22.2.15.	Preparing for Embarkation. 7 L.h. received.	
23.2.15.	do. do. 6 H.h. handed to 1/2 N. Mid Bde F.A. Large quantity of stores received fr. Ordnance. Amelot received 9 wagons G.S. Mk X. Orders re composition } 1st Batty. — 1 wagon G.S. Mk X. of train received }	
24.2.15.	Stores coming in fr. Ordnance well, & units rapidly being completed	

40

DATE	SUMMARY OF EVENTS AND INFORMATION	REMARKS REFERENCE APPENDICES
26.2.15	Brigade due to leave Bishops Stortford as under for FRANCE to join Expeditionary Force as part with Division.	
	1. 3/4 of 2nd Battery at 4.10 am. — left at 4.20 am.	
	2. 1/4 do do + 1/2 1st Battery at 5.40 am — 6.45 am	
	3. Am. Col. at 7.10 am — 8.35 am.	
	4. H.Qrs + 1/2 1st Battery. at 8.40 am — 9.20 am.	
	1. Due to arrive at Southampton in above order at 9.30 am	
	2. — 11. am.	
	3. — 12.30 pm	
	4. — 2 pm.	
	1 Arrived in above order at 9.45 am.	
	2 — 11.30 am.	
	3 — 1.46 pm.	
	4 — 3.30 pm.	
	On arrival at Southampton each trainload embarked vehicles — the horses then went to Rest Camp for the night. Officers billeted in town. All arrangements smooth.	

HOW DATE PLACE	SUMMARY OF EVENTS AND INFORMATION	REMARKS REFERENCE APPENDICES
26.2.15.	Orders received at 9.p.m to embark tomorrow as under	
27.2.15	Sailed at embarkation carried out 2 Batty 1/21st Batty at at time ordered. Amb't at 7 a.m 5 p.m.	
3.p.m.	Head quarters 1 Batty at 10 a.m. Sailed at 3¼ p.m	

H.Q. & ½ 1st Batty all embarked in 1 hr and 15 mins.
1 Rider rejected by Vet. at embarkation shed as lame.
Lieut. Col. Gisborne is O.C. Troops on board S.S. PANCRAS
which sails with following troops.

	Officers	Others	Horses	G.S.&Vehicles	2w	Bikes Gus
H.Q. & ½ 1st Battery	7	108	98	3	5	1 2
2/1 N.Mid. Co. R.E.	3	95	32	3	4	— 17 —
1/2 4th Lincolns	3	52	36	3	7	2 10 — x 1 motor cycle

Also on board 4½ tons Ordnance stores, ½ ton stationary.
S.S. PANCRAS steamed to anchorage near Guard ship when she dropped anchor.
Orders issued to troops for discipline, ration & forage drawing and emergency stations stood to & troops shewn how to put on lifebelts & when same kept - parties told off to same celerity &c.

42

HOW DATE PLACE	SUMMARY OF EVENTS AND INFORMATION	REMARKS REFERENCE APPENDICES
	Allotments explained & given to O.C. units with ref to instructions received fr. Embarkation Officer.	
	Cypher key word for voyage received fr. Embarkation Officer.	
28.2.15	Still lying off Guard Ship at Southampton.	
	No casualties & have much comfortable orat ions round correctly — something satisfactory.	
11.30 a.m.	Colonel inspected units onboard & visited horse boxes & men's sleeping places etc.	
	Saddles removed last night as it seemed a pity to keep weight on backs knowing we should not sail for 24 hrs at least.	
6.30 p.m. 5.45 p.	Sailed. A good voyage — no casualties.	

121/4808.

A2
A96

46th
North Midland Division

1/4th N.M. How: Bde: RFA.

Vol II 1 — 31.3.15
Nil

BRENTONNE HAVRE 1.3.15
BDE HQ PETIT POINT + PLOEGSTEERT

1.3.15

8.30am Alongside at HAVRE - began to disembark at once. it was very slow partly owing to some horses of R.E. refusing to come out blocking the brows by lying down. Also took bad about baggage in fact the mules it was last to come out.

HOUR DATE PLACE	SUMMARY OF EVENTS AND INFORMATION	REMARKS REFERENCE APPENDICES
	C 2118	
2.30pm	Received orders to proceed to No 2 Rest Camp -	
5.30pm	Reached camp & found Amb'ol. already here as they crossed day before - 2nd Batty arrived with 1/2 1st Batty sometime as H.Qs & 1/2 1st Batty. All arrangements good - men settled down well. Each battery had to leave 1 officer & 30 men at Southampton owing to orders received then - this seems a pity. The splitting up of units & mixing them up with others leads to extra trouble & might cause confusion. The M.L.O. HAVRE certainly did not understand it & none of his figures agreed with ours - the proper ones.	
2.3.15 12.noon.	Received orders to entrain - H.Qs & 1st Batty at 3.30 pm. 2nd Batty at 7. pm. Amb'ol. at 7. pm.	44

HOUR DATE PLACE	SUMMARY OF EVENTS AND INFORMATION C 2118	REMARKS REFERENCE APPENDICES
3.3.15.	Brigade entrained as overleaf and reached STEENWERK at 4 p.m. 7 p.m. & 10 p.m. Interpreters knowing 2nd Batty & Amdot. went into billets near La MENEGATE for the night. H.Q. & 1st Batty. ordered to proceed at once to PETIT PONT to relieve 6th Siege Batty.	Block joined
4.3.15	1st Batty. occupied position by 1.30 a.m. after very hard work - very bad mud. a good deal of difficulty experienced as 6th Siege Batty. was vacating position. Position between PETIT PONT and PLOEGSTEERT. H.Q. at PETIT PONT & 1st Batty horses and wagon line. Brigade is now attached to 3rd Army Corps 4th Division. and is now disposed as follows - H.Q. & 1st Batty as above.	
5.30 p.m.	1 Sect. 2nd Batty near 1st Batty on S. of road. 1 Sect. do near L'EBIZEE attached to 14th F.A.B. Amdot. near La MENEGATE	
	2nd Army Comdr. Genl. Sir Horace Smith Dorrien 3rd Corps Comdr. Genl. Pulteney. 4th Division. Major Genl. Wilson C.R.A. Brig. Genl. Fox	

DATE	SUMMARY OF EVENTS AND INFORMATION C.2118	REMARKS REFERENCE APPENDICES
4.3.15 Cont.	Whole day occupied in making gun platforms - laying out lines & B's going to observation posts & sets communication going.	
5.3.15	1st Batty registered in also did 2nd Batty sec. at PETITPONT Observation post of 1st Batty & billet of H.Qrs both shelled today so Brigade may be said to have received it's baptism of fire. Lieut Newton & Lieut. S.S. HASLAM & 60 gunners left behind at SOUTHAMPTON rejoined last night. Major Pat Nickalls S.M.D.R.F.A. attached to 2nd Batty. Lieut. Strakes R.F.A. attached 1st Batty from 32nd Brigade 2nd Lt. Balcomb Brown R.F.A. — 2nd Batty fr. DAC 4th Division.	
6.3.15	Situation unchanged. Brigade co-operates with 10th & 11th Infty B'de fronts.	
7.3.15	Situation unchanged.	
8.3.15	Situation unchanged. Major Nickalls left for England.	
9.3.15	Situation unchanged.	
10.3.15	Situation unchanged.	
11.3.15	Situation unchanged.	
12.3.15	do do.	

HOUR DATE PLACE	SUMMARY OF EVENTS AND INFORMATION C 2118	REMARKS REFERENCE APPENDICES
13.3.15.	Situation unchanged.	
14.3.15	Situation unchanged. 84th Infantry Brigade arrive to relieve 10th Infty BP.	
15.3.15.	Situation unchanged. 84th Infty Brig. relieves 10th Infty Brig. night of 15/16th	
16.3.15.	Re-arrangement of 5th & 4th Divisions. Brigade less 1 sec. 2nd truly Batty at LE BIZET passes under orders of 2nd Corps. 1 sec 2nd truly Batty. remains with 14th F.A.B. Ammunition supplied by N.M.&A.C. attached 5th D.A.C. at St JANS CAPPEL and 2nd Park at FLETRE.	Ap. 1 & Ap. 1A.
17.3.15.	The above re-arrangement of troops was cancelled and Ap. 1 & Ap 1A destroyed. Situation unchanged.	
18.3.15.	do do	
19.3.15	do do.	
20.3.15	do do	
21.3.15.	do do	
22.3.15	do do.	

Date	Summary of Events and Information	Remarks Reference Appendices
23.3.15.	No change.	
24.3.15.	Situation unchanged	
25.3.15	do do	
26.3.15.	do do.	
27.3.15.	do. do. Gen Sir Horace Smith-Dorrien visited the Brigade.	
28.3.15.	do do	
29.3.15.	do do	
30.3.15	do do.	
31.3.15.	do do.	

121/5/161

North Midland Division

4th N.M. (Stos²) Bde RFA.

Vol III 1 - 30.4.15

SECRET.

1/4 North Midland Howitzer Brigade
R.F.A. "T".

WAR DIARY

From   APRIL 1st 1915

           to

               APRIL 30th 1915.

H.A.Whichelow.
Major R.F.A.
Adjutant
1/4 N.M. Hows.

DATE PLACE	SUMMARY OF EVENTS AND INFORMATION C 2118	REMARKS REFERENCE APPENDICES
1915.		
April 1.	Situation unchanged.	
— 2. 4.30 p.m.	Situation unchanged. 2/Lt Spurrier and 2/Lt Joyes joined from 2/4th N.M. How. Bde. for duty — their arrival due to an application for a 3rd subaltern for battery. The old establishment allowed of 3 subs. per battery but this was reduced to 2. in Nov./14. which is inadequate. 2/Lt Balcombe-Brown & Lt Stroker attached for duty since 5.3.15 both left the Brigade end of March. Received orders that Brigade would vacate present positions & hand over to Howitzer Brigade South Midland Division next week.	
— 3.	Situation unchanged. Officers of S.M. How. Bde arrived to see positions	
— 4.	do. do. Bde Comds & both Batty Comds. to reconnoitre new positions.	
— 5th	do. do.	
— 6. 10 p.m.	1st Batty. vacated old positions — joined at NEUVE EGLISE by 4 wagons of Am. Col. & proceeded to new position together. New position in 5th Division area near KEMMEL about 6 miles N.E. of BAILLEUL. Battery is detached & for tactics is under Colonel Lawson Gower 3rd N. Md. Bde. R.F.A. "T"	49

DATE HOUR	SUMMARY OF EVENTS AND INFORMATION C2118	REMARKS REFERENCE APPENDICES
6th 2.p.m.	Headquarters handed over to South Midland Howitzer Brigade, and moved to new billets near LOCRE - between LOCRE and BAILLEUL	
5.30p.m	2nd Early Battery & 4 wagon ammunition Column moved to new position near NEUVE EGLISE - this battery is under Colonel Tongue & attached to 1st N. Mid. F.A. Brigade for tactical purposes. The above arrangement from a Brigade point of view is a most unsatisfactory one as it leaves Brigade Commander without a tactical command.	
	The Brigade is now part of 2nd Corps. 2nd Army and temporarily attached to 6th Division pending the taking over of 5th Div. line by North Midland Division.	
7th	Situation unchanged.	
8th	do do.	
9th	do. do. C.R.A.N.M.D. takes over command of N.M.Div Arty which is now in action having taken over positions of 5th Div Arty.	
10	Situation unchanged	

50

HOUR DATE PLACE	SUMMARY OF EVENTS AND INFORMATION	REMARKS REFERENCE APPENDICES
11th	Situation unchanged.	
12th	~~Bde~~ Batteries remain in same positions but under tactical control of Brigade Commander as well as for administrative purposes. Brigade in support of Infantry Brigades of N.M. Division. Divisional Commander visited Bde. HQs. Situation unchanged. Zeppelin passed over HQs. Brigade Billet 11.30 p.m. having been to BAILLEUL where it dropped bombs.	
13th	do. do.	
14th	do. do.	
15th	do. do.	
16th	do. do.	
17th	do. do. Heavy firing took place all night commencing 7.45 p.m. on our front - this in conjunction with operations further north.	
18th	Situation unchanged.	
19th	do. do.	
20th	do. do.	
21st	do do	

Date	Summary of Events and Information	Remarks Reference Appendices
	C2118	
22nd.	Situation unchanged. Some big shells on ridge near 2nd Batty position.	
23rd.	Situation unchanged on our front but Germans more active - fighting heavy North of YPRES	
24th.	Fighting continues N. of YPRES. Germans said to have crossed canal in two places yesterday between French & Canadians. On our front though nothing important has taken place it is somewhat more active and Germans are shelling trenches pretty severely at times.	
25.	Situation unchanged.	
26.	do. do. German artillery on our trenches more active.	
27	do. do. Germans shelled WULVERGHEM heavily in afternoon.	
28	do. do.	
29.	do. do. all quiet.	
30.	do. do. NEUVE EGLISE shelled.	

121/5556

46th Division

1/4th NM (Hos') Bde RFA.

Vol IV 1 — 31.5.15

DATE	SUMMARY OF EVENTS AND INFORMATION C2118	REMARKS REFERENCE APPENDICES
1915.		
May 1.	Situation unchanged.	
2.	" "	
3	" " Captain Sadler joins vice Lt Newton as vet officer. Captain Sadler was always with the Brigade since its formation but on outbreak of war went to the Front with A.S.C.	
4	Situation unchanged. Major Webber Adjutant ordered to LAHORE DIV. Departure to take place when relieved by another Adjutant.	
5	Lieut Newton RVC leaves Brigade for duty with Div. Amn Column.	
6	Situation unchanged. Capt. Archdale posted as Adjutant.	
7	Situation unchanged. (with effect from 7.5.15. Lt Whaley sick to Base Hospital	
8	" "	
9	" " Mine exploded by us at 7 p.m. caused some shelling of our trenches.	
10	" " Both batteries registered targets with aeroplane observation.	
11	" "	
12	" "	
	" "	

Date Place	Summary of Events and Information	Remarks Reference Appendices
1915	C 2118	
May 14	Situation unchanged.	
15	" " Enemy's guns on our front slightly more active.	
16	" "	
17	" "	
18	" "	
19	" "	
20	" "	
21	" "	
22	" "	
23	" "	
24	" "	
25	" "	
26	" " Capt. A.S. Archdale RFA posted from Adjutant 4th N.M. Bde to adjutant 15 Bde RFA. Lt. H. W.H. Armytage posted to 4th N.M. Bde. vice Capt. Archdale	
	" "	

HQ DATE PLACE	SUMMARY OF EVENTS AND INFORMATION	REMARKS REFERENCE APPENDICES
MAY 28th	Situation unchanged. (Capt A.S. Archdale leaves for 15th Bde RFA. Lt Armytage taking over as Adj 4th N.M. How Bde.	HQ
— 29th	" " Weather good	HQ
— 30th	" " " "	HQ
31st	" " " "	HQ

H Armytage
Lt RFA.

Lionel Pilson Lt. Col.
Cmdg. 1/4 N.M. How. Bde. R.F.A.(T)

121/6695

46th Division

1/4 N.M. Bde R.F.A.
Vol VII
1 - 31. 5. 15

SUMMARY OF EVENTS AND INFORMATION
4th N M Bde RFA

Remarks / Reference to Appendices

Sun Aug 1st — Very quiet day. F.G.C.M. on 2.2.3 Spencer & Gr Wheatly, both cases dismissed.
2nd Battery had combined shoot with a trench mortar at trenches on Hill 60.

Mon Aug 2nd — Very quiet day. 2nd Battery retaliated on to German trenches at request of 4th Lincs Regt, whose Hqs were being heavily shelled.
1st Battery retaliated over trench 50 & so stopped the enemy trench mortaring 20.50.

Tues Aug 3rd — A few light shrapnel shells burst round first battery gun position at 3.15 A.M.
2nd Battery finished burying cable.

Wed Aug 4th — Very quiet day, practically no hostile shelling in our Zone. 1st & 2nd Batteries had a combined shoot at a trench mortar.
At 6 P.M. 2nd Battery began to knock down a

DATE	SUMMARY OF EVENTS AND INFORMATION	Remarks References Appendices
	section of the enemies parapet (orders from C.R.A.) 50 rounds were allowed for us. Only 10 rounds were got off before dark, but last shot found range & line. Capt Whaly rejoined Brigade from England.	44h.
Aug 5th	A quiet day. Very little hostile shelling in our immediate zone. O.C. 2nd D:B fired 60 rounds at an earthwork I 30 b 3.6. Result parapet damaged.	
6.8.15	At 3 a.m. enemy fired a number of shells in vicinity of 1st Batt. position. O.C. 2nd D B fired 76 rounds at I 30 b 36 result not very satisfactory with exception of 1 gas cylinder exploded.	

Date	SUMMARY OF EVENTS AND INFORMATION	Remarks References Appendices
7.8.15	A quiet day. Five gunners joined from Base: 2 to 1st Battery, 1 to 2nd Battery & 2 to A.C.	
8.8.15	A quiet day.	
9.8.15	" " YPRES bombarded with heavy shell. Bombarded enemy trenches for 40 mins in conjunction with 6th Division. 1st Battery zone 48-A 2nd Battery zone trenches behind 49 & 50.	
10.8.15	A quiet day. YPRES again bombarded.	
11.8.15	" " " " "	
12.8.15	1st Battery and No. 2 Wagon lines moved to H.15 a.1.0. to make room for some heavy guns.	Corpl Henson (A.C.) wounded while in charge of wire digging party.
13.8.15	A quiet day.	
14.8.15	" " "	

DATE	SUMMARY OF EVENTS AND INFORMATION	Remarks References Appendices
15.8.15	1 Section No 5 Mountain Battery under Lt. Christie came into position at FRENCH HOUSE & came under our Command for tactical purposes.	
16.8.15	YPRES heavily bombarded for about 1 hour morning & evening.	
17.8.15	Gunner LUCK joined from N.M Base depot. Posted to 1st D.B.	
18.8.15	Situation normal.	
19.8.15	" "	
20.8.15	" "	
21.8.15		21.8.15. Sergt Manning & Driver Parsley proceeded on 7 days & 1 month leave respectively
22.8.15	Sergt Major Hardy W., Sergt Jenkes and two gunners joined from Base. 1st Batt take over zone A3 & 41A (inc) night 22nd/23rd.	

DATE	SUMMARY OF EVENTS AND INFORMATION	Remarks References Appendices
23.8.15	Situation normal. 2nd Batt. take over zone 41A exclusive to 33 inclusive night 23/24th.	Bomb.r Dobson O.H. 2nd Batt. wounded while mending telephone wire.
24.8.15	2nd Batt fired 12 rounds at Hill 60.	
25.8.15	Head Quarters turned out by 3rd S.ir move to H.24 b 9.2.	
26.8.15	Situation normal.	
27.8.15	Command of Brigade taken over by Major Drury Lowe during Col. Fisbourne's leave. 25 shrap. rounds 3de H.d 2r at 8 p.m.	a/Bomb.r Found K.S 1st Batt. wounded while mending telephone wires Col Fisbourn proceeded on leave (7 days) Sergt Major C Hardy proceeded on leave (7 days).
28.8.15 (Sat)	Gunner A. Chorley receives notification of grant of testimonial by Royal Humane Society for life saving.	
29.8.15	Situation normal	
30.8.15	KRUISSTRAT heavily shelled between 2 & 4 p.m. Capt Armytage rejoins from Base.	

HOW DATE PLACE	SUMMARY OF EVENTS AND INFORMATION	Remarks References Appendices
31.8.15	Situation normal.	

[signature]
Major for Lieut. Col., R.F.A., "T."
Commanding 1/4th North Midland (Howitzer) Brigade, R.F.A. "T."

12/5935.

46th Division

1/4th N.M. (Staintzey) Bde R.F.A.

Vol V 1 — 30.6.16.

HOUR DATE PLACE	SUMMARY OF EVENTS AND INFORMATION	REMARKS REFERENCE APPENDICES
DRANOUTRE		
June 1st	Situation on our front normal. Weather fine, light & good	JtG
2nd	" " " " " " " " " " "	JtG
3rd	" " " " " " " " " " "	JtG
4th	" " " " " " " " " " V.good	JtG
5th	" " " " " " " " " " "	JtG
6th	" " " " " " " " " " "	JtG
7th	" " " " " " " " " very hot " "	JtG
8th	" " " " " " V. sultry morning thunderstorm in the afternoon	JtG
9th	" " " " " " " " & rain	JtG
10th	" " " " " V. misty all day rain in the evening	JtG
11th	'C' trenches heavily crumped in the morning. Weather cool & fine	JtG
12th	C " again shelled 2nd Bty retaliated " " N. wind	JtG
13th	C " " " . Cold evening strong N. wind	Lt Col Gisborne & Capt MacMichael proceed home on 5 days leave JtG
14th	Nothing doing. Weather fine. Capt Walkden & Lt Haslam attached to 4th Northumbrian Bde at Ypres	JtG
15th	" "	JtG
	Between 3 p.m. & 6 p.m. the Division made a slight demonstration in support of an attack against BELLEWARDE Farm east of Ypres. J3 trench was blown up the night before & J & K trenches heavily bombarded with trench mortars. However no ground was lost	JtG

DATE	PLACE	SUMMARY OF EVENTS AND INFORMATION	REMARKS REFERENCE APPENDICES

DRANOUTRE

June Thurs. 17th — Weather good. Situation normal — HQ
Fri. 18th — " " — HQ
Sat. 19th — East wind v. cold " — HQ
Sun. 20th — Warmer " Capt Weekdens & Haslam return from Ypres & Eddowes 5 days leave. Major Crompton started for 5 days leave
Mon. 21st — Fine day. Adj & Capt of one of the 4th Northumbrian Bde RFA arrived & were shewn over the positions & observing stations. Lts Newton & Haslam left with a section of the 1st Bty at 8.45pm & went to a position one mile North of DICKEBUSCH preparatory to going into action North of ZILLEBEKE Lake.
Tues. 22nd — Fine day. Situation normal. — HQ
Wed. 23rd — Warm morning. One section of the 2nd Bty was relieved by Northumbrian Bde at 9pm & marched to a position in reserve 1½ miles North of BOESCHEPE accompanied by sub-section of A.C. under command of Capt MacDudsell & 2/Lt Dufton respectively — HQ
Thurs 24th — Quiet day. Rear sections of 1st & 2nd Bty & A.C. were relieved at 9pm & marched to reserve position getting in by 2am — HQ

HOUR DATE PLACE	SUMMARY OF EVENTS AND INFORMATION	REMARKS REFERENCE APPENDICES
BOESCHEPE		
Fri, June 25th	Position reconnoitred by C.O. & Capt MacDuibhall for 2nd Bty to come into action under orders of C.R.A. 14th Division. Position selected, J 15 d 3.5 } Sheet 28 Wagon lines H 21 c 2.2 }	N of Zillebeke Road N of Dickebusch J.M.S.
Sat, June 26	Major W Furney-Lowe, Lieut Armytage R.F.A. and Capt Greaves R.A.M.C.T. proceeded on leave 26th – 30th June. 2nd Battery and a complete Section of the Am. Column left at 7 A.M. from L 34 c 4.2 and L 28 c 2.6 Sheet 27. Section of the Am. Column received orders to move from G.O.C. R.A. 14th Division, and have today moved to J 17 c 3.4 two miles N of Reninghelst	J.M.S.
Sun, June 27th	Nothing doing. Bomb. Gunn 347 wounded (2nd Battery)	J.M.S.

58

DATE PLACE	SUMMARY OF EVENTS AND INFORMATION	REMARKS REFERENCE APPENDICES
Mon June 28th	Nothing doing.	JMS
Tues June 29th	Rear positions reconnoitred by C.O., position selected H 18 d 7.8. 2nd Battery attached 14th Div.	
Wed June 30th	Nothing doing	JMS
Thurs July 1st		

H. Wyther
Capt. R.F.A.
Adjt 1/4th N.M. (How) Bde R.F.A.

Lionel Gisborne
Lieut. Col. R.F.A.
Commanding 1/4th N.M. (How) Bde. R.F.A.

<u>Confidential.</u>

War Diary
of
1/4th North Midland (Howitzer) Bde. R.F.A.T.

from 1.6.15 to 30.6.15.

Lionel Lister
Lieut. Col. R.F.A.T.
Commanding 1/4th North Mid. (How.) Bde
R.F.A.T.

46th Dragoons

1/4 N.M. Bde R.F.A.
Vol VII
1-31-7-15

12/6243

HOUR DATE PLACE	SUMMARY OF EVENTS AND INFORMATION	Remarks Reference Appendices
BOESCHEPE & YPRES		
THURS July 1st	Fine day. 1st Bty under the orders of O.C. 3rd N.M. Bde RFA registered on German trenches in front of A6 East of Zillebeke. 2nd Bty attd 14th Division RA. held a zone from the YPRES–ROULERS railway on the North to the MENIN road East of HOOGE on the South. The casualties in the margin were due to one of the Bty's own shell which fell short.	KILLED IN ACTION 809 A/Bdr ORME W. 2nd Bty WOUNDED Capt E.C. MACMICHAEL 868 Gr SIMPSON
FRI " 2nd	Fine day. 2nd Bty registered German trenches on the ROULERS railway & also at the Eastern end of Railway Wood. 1st Bty registered trenches in front of A1.	Wounded on 2nd 808 Gr FISHER 1st Bty
SAT " 3rd	1st Bty shelled triple line of trenches opposite A6 with good result. 2nd Bty registered BELLEWARDE Farm & shelled DEAD MAN'S BOTTOM & also trenches North of HOOGE	Proceeded on leave Capt G.G. WALKDEN 1st Bty Lt E.S. HASLAM 2nd Bty 20579 BSM MOORE G. 1486 Gr RICE A.W. 1st Bty

HOUR DATE PLACE	SUMMARY OF EVENTS AND INFORMATION	Remarks Reference Appendices
YPRES		
SUN JULY 4th	Zones of Batteries changed 1st Bty to take on trenches A9 – A2, 2nd Bty A3 to A12. The day was spent in altering gunpits to enable this to be done. Very little could be done by daylight owing to hostile aeroplanes & so only the 1st Bty fired. Batteries were handed back to the Brigade at 6pm	AH
MON – 5th	Commn established with trenches of the new zone, all observations must be done from the trenches. Both batteries registered in the afternoon. Fine warm day.	Bde HQ established in dugouts in the Bund at the N.W. corner of ZILLEBEKE TANK AH
TUE – 6th	At 6.45 am Batteries registered & demonstrated in one. Points fired at were the group of trenches opposite A12 the trenches in CLONMEL COPSE opposite A8 the three lines of trenches opposite A6 & the network of trenches opposite A1 & A2. A fine day	AH WOUNDED 876 G/r HUNT J.B.

HOUR DATE PLACE	SUMMARY OF EVENTS AND INFORMATION	Remarks Reference Appendices
YPRES		
WED JULY 7th	Fine day, nothing doing. Neither Bty fired but telephone commun: to trenches duplicated. 1st Bty running wires to 49 & A1. 2nd Bty to A6 & A9 from which trenches the front can be properly covered. Rain in the afternoon	HQ
THURS " 8th	Fine morning rain again in the afternoon. Our front was quiet & the Batteries did not fire. Gun positions shelled with light shrapnel & pcs	HQ
FRI " 9th	1st Bty fired at commun: trenches opposite 49 trench & the network of trenches opposite A1. 2nd Bty registered & fired at trenches opposite A2 & A6 & at the Southern of CLONMEL Copse for purposes of retaliation & demolition. Weather good. Bde H.Q. dugouts & 2nd Bty gun positions shelled with light shrapnel & "White Swans" (5"9)	HQ Proceeded on leave No 361 BS SMITH J. 1st Bty

HOW. DATE PLACE	SUMMARY OF EVENTS AND INFORMATION	Remarks References Appendices
YPRES		
SAT. JULY 10th	Fine day. 2nd Bty did not fire but 1st Bty shelled the network of trenches opposite A1 & did some damage to the parapets. Bde HQ again shelled this time with 5.9" shrapnel & H.E. O.P's for ground behind our trenches were reconnoitred.	Capt A.P. NICHOL joined from D.A.C. posted to /b A.C. Proceeded on leave Lt. H.L. NEWTON
SUN JULY 11th	A cold day. Considerably more shelling on the part of the enemy all over the country between Ypres & the trenches. 2nd Bty registered North corner of CLONMEL copse & the trenches just North of it. O.P's covering ground immediately in rear of our trenches in case the Infantry were driven back were completed during the night.	Proceeded on leave Lt G.D. WILSON H.G. 876 Gr HUNT J.E returned from hospital
MON JULY 12th	Neither Bty fired during the day. At 7.15 p.m. the enemy blew up part of ~~Huth~~ Trench 50 & this trench was subjected to a very heavy trench mortaring for about 10 minutes 1st & 4th N.M. Bde HQ shelled between 4 & 4.15 p.m.	H.G.

HOW DATE	SUMMARY OF EVENTS AND INFORMATION	Remarks Reference Appendices
VPRES TUE. JULY 13th	5th Division are being relieved on this front by another brigade of the 46th. 138th Inf Bde relieving the 15th Inf Bde. 2nd Bty are to move their position to 127 a 9.6. Three guns in one hedge & one gun a little in rear. From here they are to cover from 35 Trench to 47 trench the 1st Bty will cover from 48 to A12. Neither Bty fired during the day. Bde HQ & 2nd Bty were shelled by 5.9" at 4.30 pm	HG 2Lt W.S. KENNEDY joined for 14 days instruction from 2/4 Lowland Bde RFA T'
WED. " 14th	Nothing doing all day. Weather was good at 8 p.m. 1st Bty fired two rounds at enemy trenches in front of 50 & 2 in retaliation to hostile. 2nd Bty moved into new position 11.30 pm	HG Cpl H. LEWIS joined & posted to 2nd Bty.
THURS " 15th	1st Bty fired in front of 48 49 & 50 trenches in retaliation to German shell fire. A few shell round Bde HQ & 2nd Bty during the afternoon. 2nd Bty ~~moved into the~~	Proceeded on leave HG 393 Sgt CRANE W 2nd Bty

64

	SUMMARY OF EVENTS AND INFORMATION	Remarks References Appendices
YPRES		
FRI. JULY 16TH	~~ration at 11.30 pm~~ registered in front of 35 trenches Very quiet day rained all night. 2nd Bty continued registration, registered the CATERPILLAR	Proceeded on leave Lt J.H.N CATTLE
SAT " 17TH	Rained all night. Combined shoot arranged with 23rd Bde between 1st Bty, 129th Bty RFA (4.5" Hows) & 18pdr against a working party on the German trenches in front of 12 O up to B 3 but 1st Bty's wires were cut. At 11 am 1st Bty fired 20 rounds at the German trenches opposite A 2 O A 5 considerable damage was done to rear trenches. 2nd Bty fired at the distant barrier of sandbags across the Railway cutting behind Hill 60 doing damage Lieut Armytage Adjutant went into Hospital.	Proceeded on leave 410 Cpl ORCHARD H H.Q

65

HOW DATE	SUMMARY OF EVENTS AND INFORMATION	Remarks Reference Appendices
Ypres		
Mon July 19	Fine day rather windy. 1st Battery fired one round at trench opposite A 6. 2nd Battery fired at working party on Western slope of Hill 60 at 9 p.m. by request of Brigade Major 138th Inf Bde. Lt H.L. Newton reported at Hqs to act as Adjutant	Proceeded on Leave Lgt Potter J.M.S.
Tues July 20	at 7.5 P.M. 2nd Battery fired 14 rounds at trenches on Hill 60 on the order from C.R.A, with satisfactory result. Between 4.30 a.m and 6.30 a.m Enemy shelled S.W. side of Zillebeke Lake, with large high explosive and Shrapnel. A good many of these fell close to 1st Battery Position. At 11.45 a.m 1st Battery fired 6 rounds at Y 5 3. Reason aggression.	Killed in action Gunner Tolleday HLN

99

	SUMMARY OF EVENTS AND INFORMATION	Remarks Reference Appendices

At 11.7 a.m. 2nd Battery fired 86 rounds at
The Caterpillar, and at 2.44 10 rounds
at enemy's gun position, located by
flashes at T.25.c.2.1
Situation fairly quiet.

Wed July 21st Between 8.30 P.M. & 10.30 P.M. Enemy shelled
ground close to Hqs & 1st Battery very
heavily, principally with Shrapnel.
At 2.15 2nd Battery fired 10 rounds at
trenches on reverse slope of Hill 60
At 5.15 1st Battery fired 10 rounds at
Communication trench between Y 58 & Y 60.
A draft of 1 officer (2nd Lieut Heaton) and
15 men arrived at wagon lines.

HOUR DATE PLACE	SUMMARY OF EVENTS AND INFORMATION	Remarks References Appendices
Thur July 22nd	Very quiet day. 1st Battery at 3.30 P.M. fired 10 rounds at trenches near Y.50.	Proceeded on Leave 2nd Lt S. Buckham
Fri July 23rd	At 4.30 P.M. 2nd Battery fired 12 rounds at supposed gas cylinder on Hill 60. At 6.55 we exploded a small mine opposite trench 41 and at 7 P.M. a large mine opposite A 2 trenches. 1st Battery fired 9 rounds just over the crater of the latter mine.	Proceeded on Leave Lieut F. M. Joyce
Sat July 24th	At 1.45. a.m. Infantry covered by 2nd Battery reported that they were being heavily shelled. The battery retaliated with nine rounds, which had the desired effect. Between 3 P.M. & 3.30 P.M. 1st Battery position was again rather heavily shelled, with	

HOW DATE PLACE	SUMMARY OF EVENTS AND INFORMATION	Remarks Reference Appendices
	small high explosive shells & shrapnel. Two fell almost on top of Major Cramptons dug out.	
Sun Jan 25th	Church Parade was held outside the dug outs at 9.30 a.m., attended by five officers & twenty five men of Hqs Staff and 1st Battery. Two officers of the 23rd Bde also attended. A Communion Service was held in the Officers Mess afterwards. 1st Battery fired 4 rounds at mine crater opposite trench 49. 2nd Battery fired 3 rounds at enemy dug outs at I 3 b a 9 c. This fire was directed from an aeroplane by means of wireless. Third shot = target.	Proceeded on leave 2nd Robinson

HOW DATE PLACE	SUMMARY OF EVENTS AND INFORMATION	Remarks. Reference Appendices.
Mon July 26th	Very quiet day indeed. At 11 a.m. 1st Battery fired 6 rounds at trenches opposite A1. Retaliation. At 12.35 2nd Battery fired 10 rounds at trenches opposite 36 trench. Enemy retaliated on Ypres & the wood in front of 2nd Battery position. At 4.35 the 2nd Battery fired 13 rounds at a 4 gun emplacement. Observation by aeroplane. At about 6.30 a large number of high explosive shell (about 8") fell close to Ecole.	

HOW DATE PLACE	SUMMARY OF EVENTS AND INFORMATION	Remarks Reference Appendices
Tues July 27th	1st Battery fired 8 rounds at y 5·3 and support trench opposite A5. 2nd Battery fired 10 rounds at trenches on reverse slope of Hill 60, and later 14 rounds at the targets, in conjunction with aeroplane. Very quiet day. Received information that an enemy attack was likely today or tomorrow.	
Wed July 28th	Very strong wind. 8.30 a.2 enemy heavily shelled Ypres – Lille road. 1st Battery fired 27 rounds at a trench mortar.	
Thur July 29th	Very quiet day, neither battery fired until late at night when 1st Battery fired three rounds at request of Infantry. Last gun of 1st Battery came back from being repaired, & so the full battery is now in action.	Proceeded on Leave Lieut Spurrier.

HOW. DATE PLACE	SUMMARY OF EVENTS AND INFORMATION	Remarks Reference Appendices.
Friday July 30th	Enemy attacked near Hooge with liquid fire & took some trenches at about 3.20 a.m. 2nd Battery fired 20 rounds at 4 a.m. at enemies trenches opposite 36 at Infantry's request. At 4.20 a.m. 1st Battery fired 3 rounds at I 30 c.7.7 (trench mortar) at Infantry's request. Our counter attack (14th Division) at Hooge took place at 2.45 P.M., as a result the trenches covered by 1st Battery were trench mortared & so the Battery retaliated with 10 rounds at I 36 b 5.7. Temporary dressing station established by 14th Division outside Headquarters office. Very short of R.A.M.C. men & stretcher bearers. Our R.A.M.C. Corporal assisted & 1st Battery supplied stretcher bearers. All leave stopped.	Wounded on Leave Bomb: Hunt

HOUR DATE PLACE	SUMMARY OF EVENTS AND INFORMATION	Remarks Reference Appendices
Sat July 31st	At 12.30 A.M. enemy began bombardment from direction of Hooge.	
	At 2.45 our Infantry reported that they were being shelled & required assistance. 1st Battery fired 19 rounds and 2nd Battery 2 rounds.	
	At 3 A.M. an Infantry Sergeant reported that our Infantry needed reinforcements at once, as enemy had driven them out of Zouave Wood & were coming on through it. Reported this to C.R.A. Afterwards found this information to be untrue.	11th.
	At 12.15 A.M. received orders that 46th Division were to hold their present line at all costs.	
	From about 7 P.M. to about 9 P.M. enemy shelled all transport roads in vicinity of Zillebeke Lake, and Zillebeke Communication trench very heavily.	Killed in action Gunner Leigh.

Lieut. Col. R.F.A.
Commanding North Midland (Howitzer) Brigade, R.F.A.

12/7/21

46th Division

1/4th N.M. Bde R.F.A.
Retull
Sept. 15.

War Diary - 4th N.M. Bde R.F.A.

DATE	SUMMARY OF EVENTS AND INFORMATION	Remarks References Appendices
YPRES		
Sept 1st WED	Weather good. Situation normal	Sgt 2nd KILLED
2nd THUR	" " Wagon lines moved to H.19.d.1.2. Amm. Col. to G.22.d.2.5. 9 casualties in 2nd Bty.	No 508 BC GROUTER 473 DC SMITH E
3rd FRI	Rained heavily all day. Situation normal	WOUNDED 52 Sgt. BARKER H.
4th SAT	Rain all day on & off. 1st Bty shelled a German sap running down towards 47 trench.	440 Sgt DAVIES J.P.
5th SUN	Rain on & off all day. Nothing doing.	275 Cpl PETITT T.
6th MON	Fine day. One gun from each battery moves after dark to conspicuous spots from which to fire when enemy aeroplane or balloon is observing.	183 Gr MAWBEY A.E. 436 QBC HICKS C. 786 Gr BULLEMORE W.
7th TUE	Fine day again. After the rain during night the rear enemy barricade across the railway fell down & exposed what was supposed to be a saphead, which was fired at during the day by Second Bty. The two decoy guns fired under enemy aeroplane observation & returned after dark to their respective batteries.	1248 Gr HUNT F.G. MAJOR CRIMPTON & CAPT NICHOL went on leave.
8th WED	Fine day after wet night. 1st Bty ranged by aeroplane on ZWARTELEN Salient. 2nd Bty again fired at saphead in railway cutting	

SUMMARY OF EVENTS AND INFORMATION

YPRES

SEPT 9th THURS — Fine day. Btys fired at various points along front.

10th FRI — There was a combined bombardment of the northern edge of ZWARTELEEN Salient at midday by both batteries as well as by the 3rd Siege (6" Hows) & 15 pr batteries. In the afternoon 2nd Bty fired at an embrasure opposite 37 Rounds without much effect.

11th SAT — Fine day. Batteries did a little shooting 1st Bty retaliated against a trench mortar opposite Trench 50. 2nd Bty again fired at embrasure opposite 37 with better effect.

12th SUN — Fine day. 1st Bty obliged to register 2 guns on Hill 60 for a shoot tomorrow & at 6pm 2nd Bty fired 30 rounds at a saphead opposite 38 & 39 to enable Infantry to sink two shafts in 39 unobserved. Sap was considerably damaged.

13th MON — Fine day both batteries shoot with an aeroplane observer at midday. 1st Bty had a satisfactory shoot but 2nd Bty

HOW DATE PLACE	SUMMARY OF EVENTS AND INFORMATION	
YPRES Sept 13th MON (cont)	shoot was unsatisfactory however both Btles were given effective rounds against the huts they were firing at by observer. At 3pm there was another combined bombardment the 1st Bty firing at the Western edge of Hill 60 the 2nd Bty at the CATERPILLAR both batteries had very good results & considerable damage to enemy trenches was done.	MAJ DRURY-LOWE & CAPT WALKDEN went on leave
14th TUE	Fine day rain during night. Inf in the railway cutting were heavily shelled so 2nd Bty retaliated against CATERPILLAR & against sapland opposite 38 & 39.	
15th WED	Fine day. 1st Bty is to be attached to 3rd Division temporarily from 17th. 2nd Bty fired at a log hut opposite trench 34, into which men had been seen to go, assisted by a 15pr battery. 2nd Bty got one direct hit on hut.	CAPT NICHOL to hospital
16th THUR	Fine day nothing doing.	
17th FRI	Fine day. There was a combined bombardment between 11 am & 12 noon of the German trenches our batteries firing 50 rounds each opposite 49 & 50 doing considerable damage. In the afternoon the 2nd Bty fired 90 rounds in retaliation on 38 & 39 & 47S also the Railway Cutting were badly crumped.	

SUMMARY OF EVENTS AND INFORMATION

DATE		
SEPT 18th SAT	At noon yesterday 1st Bty passed temporarily under command of CRA 3rd Division & is allotted an area astride the YPRES-MENIN road at HOOGE up to BELLEWARDE Lake. This area was registered this morning. 2nd Bty. was ordered to take over as far as A.4 a points in the enemy line as far as trench 50 were registered. They again left to retaliate in the afternoon.	Hh
19th SUN	Tuesday wind in the East. 1st Bty joined in bombardment by 3rd Division firing 50 rounds at trenches S.W. of HOOGE CHATEAU	Hh
20th MON	Fine day wind in the south. 1st Bty registered points behind German front line about the Menin Road & in the afternoon fired 90 rounds during a bombardment of this area. 2nd Bty did not shoot.	LTS NEWTON & WILSON Hh Newton on leave
21st TUE	Fine day. 2nd Bty continued registering points taken over from 1st Bty. First Bty fired 88 rounds on trenches between HOOGE CHATEAU & the MENIN road.	Hh
22nd WED	Fine day. 2nd Bty fired some 66 rounds along the front from Hill 60 to opposite trench 50. 1st Bty fired 116 rounds at S.W. corner of HOOGE CHATEAU.	Hh

HOW		
DATE	SUMMARY OF EVENTS AND INFORMATION	
HOUR		

YPRES

SEPT 23rd THURS — 1st Bty fired 98 rounds at trenches north of MENIN road. The 2nd Bty 31 at a machine gun emplacement on Hill 60 and an embrasure opposite left of 49 with very good results.

24th FRI — Fine day. One gun from 2nd Bty went out of action last night. Between 4.20 am & 4.55 am 1st Bty fired 85 rounds at the Chateau & chateau grounds HOOGE. 2nd Bty fired 30 rounds at machine gun emplacement & embrasure opposite trench 49 during the same period. About 6pm 2nd Bty fired at a house behind Hill 60 thought to be an Observation Station. 2nd Bty gun repaired & in action after dark.

25th SAT — Fine morning between 3.50 am & 4.20 am there was a bombardment along the fronts of the 46th, 3rd & 14th Divisions followed by an attack by the 3rd Division north & south of BELLEWARDE Lake and by the 14th Division on their left. Attack was entirely successful but at 4.30 pm both divisions were forced to retire owing to a heavy bombardment. First Bty fired 618 rounds during the day & were complimented by the G.O.C. 3rd Division on their work. 2nd Bty fired 199 rounds for the day. 2nd H. Bty were covering from 34 to A6.

SUMMARY OF EVENTS AND INFORMATION

PLACE: YPRES

SEPT 26th SUN — Fine day quiet all day & guns did not fire. H.H.

27th MON — Rain on & off all day. Quiet until 10pm when two patrols met & fired at each other & then for 3/4 hour there was heavy firing on 3rd Division front. 1st Bty fired 106 rounds & were thanked by Col Elkington (O.C. Group) for their assistance. H.H.

28th TUE — Wet day. 1st Bty returned to 46th Division at midday. 2nd Bty fired 20 rounds at gun emplacement in the CATERPILLAR and embrasure opposite 49. Lt. HASLAM went on leave H.H.

29th WED — Wet day on & off. Heard that we were to come out of action at once for an unknown destination. 1st Bty came out of action at 9.30pm & was obliged to borrow 4 wagons & a limber from 2nd Bty to withdraw surplus ammn. Lt HASLAM recalled from leave. CAPT WHALEY sick to hospital

30th THUR — Rained during night but fine day with drying wind. 2nd Bty fired between 3 & 4 pm during a bombardment of the trenches B2 B3 B4 lost yesterday afternoon at 4.30pm by 3rd Division. Objectives ZWARTELEEN & Hill 60. The 2nd Bty which should have withdrawn at 9.30pm had to remain in action as mines were blown up in front of the 3rd Division, 47 trench 35 & 31 trenches & Inf were heavily shelled. 2nd Bty fired 15 rounds. H.H.

Lendl Holmes Hke and 4th How Bde RFA

H Lucy Capt RFA

85

121/7540

46th Division

1/4th N.M. Bde R.F.A.

Dec 1915

Vol IX

SUMMARY OF EVENTS AND INFORMATION

4th N.M. Bde R.H.A.

YPRES
VIEUX BERQUIN
LILLERS

Oct. 1st FRI — 2nd Bty & Brigade HQ remained in action all day. The enemy blew up another mine opposite junction of 38 & 39 but no harm was done other than a saphead destroyed. 2nd Bty withdrew to wagon lines at 8 pm & had a good night for their move.

2nd SAT — Brig HQ withdrew to H.Sqd. wagon lines. Brigade marched as part of a column at 6.10 pm night was very dark. Route via LOCRE — BAILLEUL to VIEUX BERQUIN where the Brigade arrived to find good billets at 2 am, a march of about 15 miles. — A fine night for the march but very cold. Bad checks at start owing to 9th Division being on the road.

3rd SUN — Brigade remained in billets all day which was fine & marched at 6.25 pm via MERVILLE & ROBECQ to billets in the village of LA MIQUELLERIE close to LILLERS arriving about 12.30 am after a very good march with few checks.

4th MON — Brigade remained in billets all day.

SUMMARY OF EVENTS AND INFORMATION

LILLERS & LABEUVRIERE

OCT 5th TUE — A certain amount of rain. Brigade still in billets. HQ

6th WED — Brigade moved off at 11.5 am marching via LILLERS & CHOCQUES to the village of LABEUVRIERE S.W. of BETHUNE where it arrived about 3.30 pm & was billeted in the village.

7th THURS — Brigade remained in billets & a programme of drill to be followed whilst in reserve to 11th Corps to which the Division is attached was drawn up. HQ

8th FRI — Brigade still in billets. Brigade Commander, Adj. & two Battery Commanders visited the captured German trenches in front of VERMELLES. HQ

9th SAT — Four more officers sent to visit the captured positions. Fine day. HQ

10th SUN — Fine day. 3 more officers sent to visit trenches. HQ

11th MON — Fine day. C.O. two B.C's & Adj started at 7 am & reported to C.R.A. 12th Division at LABOURSE who

SUMMARY OF EVENTS AND INFORMATION

PLACE: VERMELLES

OCT 11th MON (cont) — handed us on to C.R.A. 7th Division where we reported at 9 am. C.R.A. took C.O. & two B.C.'s to chose positions for the Batteries which were to be in houses on northern edge of village. Adj. sent back to fetch brigade into action at once. Left LABEUVRIERE at 3 pm & marched via GOSNAY — HESDIGNEUL — VAUDRICOURT — VERQUIN — VERQUIGNEUL — LABOURSE — NOYELLES-LEZ-VERMELLES — VERMELLES. Both batteries getting into action by 9 pm.
Brigade Ammunt. Col. left the Column ½ mile west of VERQUIGNEUL where it parked on the side of the road. Battery & Brigade Staff Wagon lines were chosen near the railway about ½ mile S.E of LABOURSE.
Brig Hdqrs were lent one of the few houses left standing in VERMELLES for the night.

12th TUE — A great part of the day was wasted waiting for aeroplane to register the quarries but 1st Bty

HOW	SUMMARY OF EVENTS	
DATE	AND INFORMATION	
PLACE		
VERMELLES		

OCT. 12th TUE — did some useful registration, registering PUITS 13 S.E of CITÉ ST ELIE, trench running S.E. West of CITE ST ELIE cross roads due south of this village. 2nd Bty registered trench running N.E thro' centre of HOHENZOLLERN Redoubt HQ

13th WED — 1st Bty registered trench North of QUARRIES west of CITE ST ELIE by aeroplane. 2nd Bty as well as it could by observation of 1st Bty shoot. At 12 noon bombardment began of the German line North of FOSSE NO 8 south to HULLUCH Objective of 46th Division was FOSSE NO 8 & HOHENZOLLERN Redoubt that of the 12th Division the Quarries. Both our Batteries were turned on to the same trench G60 4.5 -8.2 which runs N.W-S.E both East of the Quarries. 1st Bty only had three guns in action one having been sent to BETHUNE for repair with a broken elevating gear 2nd Bty had two guns out of action for 20 minutes. During bombardment 1st Bty fired 308 rounds 2nd Bty 303.

WOUNDED
LT. E.S. HASLAM
Gr MOORE
2nd Bty

SUMMARY OF EVENTS AND INFORMATION

VERMELLES

OCT 13th WED (cont) — The Infantry got on at first but were eventually driven back by machine gun fire from the Dump with heavy loss. The final result was that we lost BIG WILLIE & took the front trench of HOHENZOLLERN Redoubt & the trench west of the Quarries & also bombed the enemy out of the bit of Gun trench they still held.

14th THUR — A quiet day, misty. Both Batteries continued registering.

15th FRI — 2nd Bty continued registering the wall S.E. of the Dump also SLAG ALLEY. A misty day again.

16th SAT — During the night there was a certain amount of fighting. Another misty day. Batteries registered what they could PUITS 13, Slag Alley.

17th SUN — Fine, quiet day until the evening when the Batteries were called on to stop a bombing attack by the enemy. 1st Bty fired 76 rounds at trench East of Quarries & 2nd Bty 132 rounds at Slag Alley. The Guards made some progress up Big Willie bombing.

WOUNDED Capt. B.G. VALKDEN 1st Bty.

SUMMARY OF EVENTS AND INFORMATION

VERMELLES

OCT 18th MON — Fine cold day. During the day 1st Bty registered the houses in ST ELIE from which the enemy were supposed to observe & snipe into Gun Trench considerable damage was done. Considerable shelling of our trenches during the afternoon & Batteries retaliated against trench East of Quarries. About 6 pm Infantry began a bomb attack & took the square of trenches G 5 d 9.1 N.W. corner of quarries & got along trench running N.E for a short distance, also worked up from G 12 a 5.4 along QUARRY Trench for some distance. The

Oct 19th TUE — Batteries did a little firing on & off when requested by Infantry. The trench taken by bombing last night was subjected to a slow steady bombardment during the afternoon & at 5 pm enemy attacked but was repulsed with heavy loss by machine gunfire. Batteries fired 140 rounds each forming a barrage along trench G 6 c 4.5. to 8.2. between 5 pm & 7 pm. Both batteries fired 20 rounds at same target later at 9.15 pm at request of Infantry.

SUMMARY OF EVENTS AND INFORMATION

PLACE

VERMELLES

OCT 20th WED — Both batteries were called on to fire at ~~junction of communication trenches G6 d 4.5~~ trench G 6 c 4.5 to 8.2 owing to an error Infantry asking for a little fire to be brought on quarries which was translated into gunfire. 1st Bty registered point at which C.T's cross at G 6 d 4.2 West of ST ELIE. Our Infantry seem to have got on near the Quarries. They now hold the whole of Quarry trench* from G 5 d 9.0 to G 12 a 5.4 & also ~~F~~ trench from 9.0. to 2.3. ~~R~~ A misty day.

*H6 STONE ALLEY as far as pt 5.4.

21st THUR — A quiet day & finer but no good view to be obtained of enemy's lines except from front trenches. Batteries did not fire. Brigade is to come out of action tomorrow. Rain set in at 7 pm.

About 20 shells round Brewery at 4.45pm He

22nd FRI — Rained all night but cleared up in early morning & a fine day resulted. Teams ordered for 5.30pm. Brigade out of action at 6.30 pm 2nd

SUMMARY OF EVENTS AND INFORMATION

VERMELLES & LABEUVRIERE

OCT 22nd FRI (cont) Bty emptying three guns at this time. Batteries clear of VERMELLES by 6.45pm & the Brigade marched back to LABEUVRIERE by the same route as was followed in going to VERMELLES passing Battery & Column wagon lines en route the remainder joining in their proper places as the Batteries passed. Arrived at LABEUVRIERE after 2 halts at 11.30 pm a little difficulty was met by one-horsed mess carts & a few other vehicles in taking the hill out of GOSNAY but there was no real trouble.

OCT 23rd SAT Brigade in Rest Billets. Ordered to send a party of 15 including 2 officers to be attached to 61st How Bde RFA at ANNEQUIN for instruction in 4.5" Hows & with a view to taking over their guns when it is our turn in front line.

OCT 24th SUN Party for attachment left at 9am remainder busy cleaning guns etc. Fine day

OCT 25th MON Heavy rain all day

Lt J.B. PROPER joined from 2/4 Bty & posted to A/C

SUMMARY OF EVENTS AND INFORMATION

PLACE LABEUVRIERE

OCT 26th TUE — Ground very bad after yesterday's rain. Today weather considerably improved but a little rain. — Lt EDDOWES on own leave ? CC

27th WED — A little rain during the day. Bde find fatigues & clean up.

28th THUR — A party of B.C. & 2 subaltern officers & 18 men paraded at 8.15 am for an inspection by the King, marched under C.O. to the square LABEUVRIERE & from thence Dival Artillery marched under COL LEVESON-GOWER 3rd M.M. Bde RFA to the parade ground of XI Corps where markers had been posted by Adjutant. His Majesty the King accompanied by the I Army Commander rode along the front of the Corps & then after inspecting I Corps drove back past our front in his car, during the inspection of I Corps His Majesty's horse was frightened by the cheering, reared & came over on the King who was badly bruised but fortunately otherwise not injured. Brigades marched back independently

SUMMARY OF EVENTS AND INFORMATION

PLACE LABEUVRIERE

OCT 28th THUR (Cont) — Officers attending Parade, C.O., Adjt, Majors Drury-Lowe, Officers all & Crompton Lieuts. Newton, Spurrier. Parade was to some extent spoilt by rain. At 5pm a second party was sent by motorbus to relieve 1st party at ANNEQUIN.

29th FRI — Weather improved considerably, horse lines still bad but units are preparing slag standings. C.R.A. went round men's billets & lines during the afternoon.

30th SAT — A dull cold day. Nothing doing. 2/Lt S.W. WARD joined from 2/4th.

31st SUN — Dull day a little rain. Church Parade for Brigade in Horse Lines of Bde HQ at 11.40 am.

Lionel Gilstone Lt Col

Lieut. Col., R.F.A., "T."
Commanding 1/4th North Midland (Howitzer) Brigade, R.F.A. "T."

46th Division

1/4th N.M. Bde R.F.A.
Nov.
Vol X

121/7694

CONFIDENTIAL.

WAR DIARY

of

1/1st North Midland (Howitzer) Bde. R.F.A.

from 1st – 30th November

1915.

[signature]
Lieut. Col., R.F.A.,
Commanding 1/1th North Midland (Howitzer) Brigade, R.F.A.

	SUMMARY OF EVENTS AND INFORMATION	REMARKS

LABEUVRIERE

Nov 1st MON. — Wet day. Preliminary orders received to the effect that the XI Corps of which the division will form part move North & take up a line near FAUQUISSART

2nd TUE. Rained heavily all day work suspended on standings

3rd WED. Weather dull but little rain orders received to be ready to move to new area at 9 a.m. on the 4th inst. to an area S.W. of MERVILLE

4th THUR. Bde marched from LABEUVRIERE at 11.30 a.m. via CHOCQUES — GONNEHEM — ROBECQ — LES AMUSOIRES — LAHAVE to ST FLORIS which was reached at 3 p.m. Fine day all the time turning cold in the evening

5th FRI. Fine day turned foggy about 1 p.m. Bde in billets. Adjutant reconnoitred proposed Battery positions found there was no room for 1st Bty in position allotted which was reported to Bde Major

6th SAT. CRA & Bde Major met Colonels & B.C's & Adjts of 3rd & 4th Bdes & after considerable search a

HOW DATE. PLACE.	SUMMARY OF EVENTS AND INFORMATION	Remarks & reference to Appendices
NOV 7th SUN.	position was found for the 1st Bty in an orchard at M.27.a.1.1. This position will have to be made. The 2nd Bty are taking over a prepared position from 60th Bty RFA at M.32.b.5.5. Bde HQ chosen at M.35 central.	MAP REFERENCE BETHUNE Contoured 1/40,000
NOV 8th MON.	Working parties under Lt NEWTON sent from 1st Bty to get on with position & under Lt SPURRIER to clean up Bde HQ. Fine day.	Lt HEATON went on leave HQ
" 9th TUE.	Bde HQ & 2nd Bty moved off from ST FLORIS about 1pm moving via CALONNE-SUR-LA-LYS — L'EPINETTE – VIEILLE CHAPELLE to their positions in action. 2nd Bty putting two guns in action at Bty position & also relieving the flank gun	
10th WED.	Another fine day. 2nd Bty registered the DISTILLERIE S.17 central, FERME DU BOIS S.16.c.6.9. & several communication trenches. Comm's good between Bde HQ & 2nd Bty. 4th gun of 2nd Bty in action after dark.	HQ HQ

97

HOW DATE PLACE	SUMMARY OF EVENTS AND INFORMATION	Remarks References Appendices

Nov 11th THUR — Fine morning a very little rain in afternoon. 2nd Bty continued registering & did a little retaliation against the Distillery in S17c99. 1st Bty brought all guns into action in orchard at M26b91 after dark.

Nov 12th FRI. — Very high wind with rain. 1st Bty attempted to register Fme du BIEZ & house in LES BRULOT. 2nd Bty retaliated against Distillery.

13th SAT — Wind too high to allow of Registration.

14th SUN — Weather improved wind has dropped. 2nd Bty did a considerable amount of registration. A little retaliation by the enemy.

15th MON — Hard frost during the night. Ground however still wet. 2nd Bty registered several points & did a little retaliation. 1st Bty fired 20 rounds at enemy works just north of BOIS DE BIEZ known as "MUSK RAT" but with little success. — LT JOYCE went on leave.

16th TUE — Frost did not continue but day very cold. Both batteries fired a few rounds in retaliation, on to Musk Rat & Distillery.

17th WED — Frost during night. 2nd Battery front gun out of action owing to pit being flooded. — 2nd Lt Heaton failed to return from leave.

HOW DATE PLACE	Summary of Events and Information	Remarks References Appendices
18th THUR	Capt H. A. H. Armitage left Brigade. Lieut H. L. Newton reported at Hqs to act as temporary Adjutant. Lieut F. A. Joyce recommended for appointment to Adjutancy. Very cold day, some snow & rain. 2nd Battery retaliated on Distillery & Moated Farm in retaliation, by request of Centre Group. Major Crompton reconnoitred a position for 1st Battery at X.18.a.2.2, at present occupied by d.8.9 battery	LIEUT BLYTON joined the Brigade.
19th FRI	Very cold, with North East wind. Commanding Officer with Major Crompton and Adjutant went again to d.8.9 battery position to look at gun pits and O.P. 2nd Battery flank gun completed its registration from its new position.	
20th SAT	Cold and damp. 96 Piccadilly & other O.P's in Rue du Bois shelled with 4.1 How shells. 1st Battery retaliated. 2nd Battery reported a hostile Battery in action at S.23.d.1.2 and registered it	
21st Sun	Both batteries fired a few rounds as reprisal for hostile shelling of Rue du Bois. Right Section of 1st battery completed their move to X.18.d.2.2 at about 7 P.M.	

	SUMMARY OF EVENTS AND INFORMATION	Remarks & References to Appendices

22nd Mon. Very hard frost in night. 2nd Battery ordered to Huckle shelling Lieut Spurrier of O.P.s in Rue du Bois by shelling La Tourelle & the Corp Hemingway distillery. 1st Battery (right section) registered one target, but Cpl Witt & weather too misty for any further registration. Now of Gr Cuthrie left section, one gun to X.18.a.22, & the other to Pont Logie went on leave. reported complete at 6.30 P.M.

23rd Tues. Slightly warmer, but very misty. 1st Battery continued registration, & 2nd battery fired a few rounds as reprisal.

24th Wed. Much warmer day. 1st Battery practically completed registration. 2/Lieut Rowtham 2nd battery fired a few rounds in reply to enemy shelling arrived to be of Rue du Bois. Between 10 P.M. & 12 P.M. 2nd battery had attacked the 2nd a combined shoot with 18 pdrs at the Orchard (S.11.a.8.7). Battery for 14 day

25th Thurs. Warm day. West wind. 2nd battery F.O.O. reported that as a result of 18 pdr shelling, some Germans left their trenches & retired across the open, behind the Rauen Head. 2nd battery fired a few rounds at them. Between 1 P.M. & 1.45 P.M. both batteries fired 40 rounds at german trenches & Ferme du Bois, taking part in a general bombardment.

Hour & Date Place	Summary of Events and Information	Remarks References Appendices
28.11.15	Fine cold morning good light. 1st Batty fired 20 rounds at Cour d'Avoué, two direct hits on building. 2nd Batt fired 12 rounds on Distillery	2/Lt Healon returned from leave
29.11.15	Frost turned to rain dull day bad light. rain continued all day. 1st Batty fired 25 rds on Ferme du Bois, 2nd Batty fired 24 rds on houses N.W. of La Tourelle cross roads and 20 rounds later at the same target	
30.11.15	Fine warm morning. Enemy shelled near 2nd Batty flank gun wounding one man Gnr Simms. 1st Batty 2 P.M. 25 rounds at Rue du Marais S 22 c 5.7. 3 P.M. 1st Batty 25 rounds at S 16 a 6.4 (Flank Gun). 2nd Batty fired 32 rounds in reprisals	Lt Spencer returned off leave.

Lionel Potter Lt Col

Date Place	Summary of Events and Information	Remarks References Appendices
25/11/15	Copy of opperation order No 1. Lieut F. M. Joyce returned off leave and took over the duties of adjutant from Lieut H. L. Newton who performed duties whilst Lt Joyce was on leave. Lt Joyce's appointment dated from November 18th 2/Lt Heaton granted extension of leave from 16th to 25/11/15 authority (W.O.)	filed
26/11/15	Snow in morning very cold. 1st Batt registered 2 guns on S 23 d 1.1 mist and snow made observation difficult. 2nd Batt registered pump at S 11 b 9.1. At 12 midnight 2nd Batt fired 25 rounds at Boars Head. 2/Lieut Burra reported to colonel. 7.30 PM to 9.30 PM. 1st Battery fired 32 rounds at Ferme-du-Bois	Lt Haslam W.K. Cpl Lakin Br Nobel Dr Oday went on leave to ENGLAND
27/11/15	Morning fine and frosty. 2nd Battery registered strong point S 16 a 9½.8 firing 13 rounds also registered flank gun on distillery and La Tourelle X roads firing 16 rounds. At 12 noon 1st Battery fired 20 rounds at M.G. emplacement near Ferme du Bois. A large % of blinds was noticed in enemy's shells.	

CONFIDENTIAL.

WAR DIARY.

1/4th: NORTH MIDLAND BRIGADE. R.F.A. 46

DECEMBER 1st: to 31st: 1915.

Vol XI

Army Form C. 2118.

WAR DIARY
or
INTELLIGENCE SUMMARY
(Erase heading not required.)

Instructions regarding War Diaries and Intelligence Summaries are contained in F. S. Regs., Part II. and the Staff Manual respectively. Title pages will be prepared in manuscript.

Hour, Date, Place	Summary of Events and Information	Remarks and references to Appendices
1.12.15	Rain early turned fine later. 1st Batty fired 25 rounds at FERM DU BOIS and 20 rounds at Enue S23 b 2/2.6 good results from both shoots. 2nd Batty fired 21 rounds on works near farm S236.2½.5½ obtaining direct hit, also 20 rounds on strong point S170.2.7 with little effect.	
2.12.15	Fine warm morning. Lt Col Girdwood started on leave. At 2.P.M. 1st Batty fired 25 rounds on distillery causing a considerable amount of damage, very satisfactory shoot. At various times during the day 2nd Batty engaged the distillery. Leave cancelled all Officers to be recalled. Sent wire to Lt Col Girdwood and Lt W.K's Hazlam. 11.P.M. received orders by wire to entrain on 6th and 7th inst. Warned all units. Pouring wet night.	Major Drury - have assumed temporary command of Brigade
3.12.15.	Wet dull morning. Aim was too misty to carry out artillery program. 2nd Batty fired 18 rounds on distillery. Left Section of 1st Batty was relieved at 9.30 P.M. by a Section of D Batty of 89th Bde R.F.A. 19th division, and proceeded to its new billeting area P14 a. 5.3. 2nd Batty right Section was relieved at 8.30 P.M. by a Section of C Batty 89th Bde R.F.A. 19th division and proceeded to its new billeting area P14 a. 7.3.	

Army Form C. 2118.

WAR DIARY
or
INTELLIGENCE SUMMARY.
(Erase heading not required.)

Instructions regarding War Diaries and Intelligence Summaries are contained in F. S. Regs., Part II. and the Staff Manual respectively. Title pages will be prepared in manuscript.

Hour, Date, Place	Summary of Events and Information	Remarks and references to Appendices
4.12.15	1st Batty left section arrived at new billets P14 a 5.3 at 4.0 A.M. 2nd Batty right section arrived at new billets P14 a 7.3 at 4.45 A.M. Drew went morning. Lt Col T Evans 89th Bde and his staff arrived at Head Quarters at 10.50 A.M. Brigade Head Quarters were Genelled at new to 89th Bde RFA at 4.0 P.M. and Head Quarters staff proceeded to their new billets at P14 a 1.2. arriving there at 10.0 P.M. Remaining section of the 1st Batty was relieved at 6.45 P.M. Remaining section of the 2nd Batty was relieved at and both proceeded to their respective new billets	
5.12.15	Remaining Section of 1st Batty arrived at new billets at 1.30 A.M. and remaining section of 2nd Batty arrived at new billets at 12.25 A.M. A great improvement in the weather. Ammn Col. were relieved by Ammn Col. of 89th Bde RFA at 11.0 A.M. and proceeded to new billets at P13 c 9.1. arriving there at 3 P.M.	Lt Col Gisborne and Lt W.K.S. Haslam returns from leave. Lt Col Gisborne granted further leave until December 13th Sadl Sgt Greenwatt Cpl. Beresford Cpl. Walz Riggs Tpr W. Reitman Dr Prim (one month) Proceeded on leave

Army Form C. 2118.

WAR DIARY
or
INTELLIGENCE SUMMARY.
(Erase heading not required.)

Instructions regarding War Diaries and Intelligence Summaries are contained in F. S. Regs., Part II. and the Staff Manual respectively. Title pages will be prepared in manuscript.

Hour, Date, Place	Summary of Events and Information	Remarks and references to Appendices
6.12.15	Fine warm morning. Turned wet later	
7.12.15	Duce wet day	
8.12.15	Fine day. G.O.C. 46th Division inspected in Field Service Marching order dismounted. The D.D.R inspected the horses of the Brigade with a view to casting. Received orders to exchange all H.D. horses of A/C and '17 wheelers H.D. and '17 leaders H.D. from each battery complete with harness.	
9.12.15	Wet day. 1st Batty exchanged 7 H.D. wheelers and 10 H.D. leaders and received 7 L.D. wheelers and 10 L.D. leaders. 2nd Batty exchanged 10 H.D. wheelers and 9 H.D. leaders and received 10 L.D wheelers and 7 L.D leaders. A/c received 2.5 mules and 29 H.D horses. All exchanges were completed with harness. Vet commanders report condition of horses and harness very bad	Craig Crompton Rotr Keays Dr Dotson Sgt Davies Cpl Price } Proceeded on short leave to England.
10.12.15	Duce wet morning. Brigade Commander attended conference at Divisional Head Quarters. Received orders that the D.D.R	

Army Form C. 2118.

WAR DIARY
or
INTELLIGENCE SUMMARY.
(Erase heading not required.)

Instructions regarding War Diaries and Intelligence Summaries are contained in F. S. Regs., Part II. and the Staff Manual respectively. Title pages will be prepared in manuscript.

Hour, Date, Place	Summary of Events and Information	Remarks and references to Appendices
10th continued	and D.V.S. were inspect the Curses of the Brigade on the 11th inst. Received orders that the Curses of the Brigade will be Inspected on Sunday next. Remainder of day very Stormy	
11.12.15	Stormy morning. D.D.R and D.V.S did not inspect horses	Gnr Kirkland Dr Longman Dr Dickinson Gnr Beer } Proceeded on Short leave to England.
12.12.15	Fine morning. Received orders to be exchanged from Batteries to CALONNE Station and to receive 43 horses from there. (1st Batty Sent 12 horses and 2nd Batty Sent 9 horses. (Horses received 42. L.D. 1 R.) Capt Hartley inspected the Curses of the Brigade.	Lt Col L G Gisborne returned off leave
13.12.15	Fine cold morning. Conference at C.R.A Office about harness received from and Resulted over to 33rd D.A.C. Horses of Brigade toiled with mallein	12/15 Maj. W.D Drury-howe 13th 12.15 Capt Crofts Bdr Cooper Gnr Bradley Gnr Wheatley } Proceeded on leave to England for 1 month To report to 3rd line at the end of leave.

(9 29 6) W 3332—1107 100,000 10/13 H W V Forms/C. 2118/10.

WAR DIARY
INTELLIGENCE SUMMARY
(Erase heading not required.)

Army Form C. 2118.

Instructions regarding War Diaries and Intelligence Summaries are contained in F. S. Regs., Part II. and the Staff Manual respectively. Title pages will be prepared in manuscript.

Hour, Date, Place	Summary of Events and Information	Remarks and references to Appendices
14.12.15	Fine cold day. Horses for casting sent to Divisional H.Q. for inspection	Cpl Ireland } 15.12.15 Bdr Booth } to 12.1.16 Proceeded to England on 1 months leave to report to O.C. 3rd line on completion. Wired Maj Drury home extended to 17.12.15
15.12.15	Fine cold day. 8 Curries from A.C. were exchanged for 8 mules. All 5" B.L. How ammunition returned to railhead in motor lorries. Received orders all 5" equipment to be put on rail at LESTREM and take over 4.5" equipment in exchange	
16.12.15	Dull morning 1st and 2nd Batty's and eight teams from A.C. proceeded to LESTREM. 874 complete rounds H.E. and 374 complete rounds of Shrapnel received in the Brigade this is 4.5" How ammunition. Returned all 5" equipment. Received 4.5" equipment in exchange.	Lieut Facer A.V.C.T. reported finished for duty. Maj Crompton returned off leave

Army Form C. 2118

WAR DIARY
or
INTELLIGENCE SUMMARY

(Erase heading not required.)

Instructions regarding War Diaries and Intelligence Summaries are contained in F.S. Regs., Part II. and the Staff Manual respectively. Title Pages will be prepared in manuscript.

Place	Date	Hour	Summary of Events and Information	Remarks and references to Appendices
In the field	17.12.15		Wet day. 2 riders and 12 L.D. horses received from D.A.C. These horses were mallein before receiving them. One of the urgent Surplus G.S. wagons handed over to D.A.C.	
	18.12.15		Duel day. Remaining 7 Surplus G.S. wagons sent to Merville and put on rail to O.O. Havre. Twits practised entraining native horses. All H.E. Selle (No 1 Gaine) exchanged for H.E. Selle (No 2 Gaine) received on Curro L.D. Brigade now up to war establishment in Curros. Major W.D. Deny have returned from leave.	
	19.12.15		Fine cold day.	B.Q.M.S. Spencer Rdr Hutley Gnr Roe proceeded on sent-leave to England 19.12.15 to 23.12.15

Army Form C. 2118

WAR DIARY
or
INTELLIGENCE SUMMARY
(Erase heading not required.)

Instructions regarding War Diaries and Intelligence Summaries are contained in F. S. Regs., Part II. and the Staff Manual respectively. Title Pages will be prepared in manuscript.

Place	Date	Hour	Summary of Events and Information	Remarks and references to Appendices
	20.12.15		Fine day. Bdr Dotson and act Bdr Found rejoined the unit	
	21.12.15		Pouring wet day. Six reinforcements received from D.A.C. and posted to 2nd Battery. Received orders to send billeting party to new area (Hamblain)	
	22.12.15		Fine morning. Lt Col Girdwood proceeded on one weeks leave from 23.12.15 to 28.12.15. Billeting Party proceeded to Hamblain and reported billets unsatisfactory	
	23.12.15		Wet morning. Maj W.D. Berry-Low assumes temporary command of the Brigade. Received orders to send advanced billeting officer to report at C.R.A Head Quarters at 8 AM on morning of 24th. Also to send officer to meet Staff Captain at the Church House Givenchy at 9.30 AM on 24th. Received orders to hand over 5 H.D. Curros from A.C. to 23rd Division artillery at K2.q.d.8.8. (Sheet 36 A) and to receive S.L.D Curros in lieu.	
	24.12.15		Fine morning. Billeting Officers each reported to his appointed place. Received orders that S.L.D. Curros received by A.C. were to be General over to 3rd Brigade. These only of the 5 H.D Curros were exchanged. Lieut Facer A.V.C returned from leave.	

1875 Wt. W593/826 1,000,000 4/15 J.B.C. & A. A.D.S.S./Forms/C. 2118.

Army Form C. 2118

WAR DIARY
or
INTELLIGENCE SUMMARY
(Erase heading not required.)

Instructions regarding War Diaries and Intelligence Summaries are contained in F.S. Regs., Part II. and the Staff Manual respectively. Title Pages will be prepared in manuscript.

Place	Date	Hour	Summary of Events and Information	Remarks and references to Appendices
In the field	25.12.15		Wet morning. Lieut H.L. Newton posted to take command of 2nd Battey. B.Q.M.S Spencer proceeded to Havre leaving provisionally selected for Mountain work. Dr Banatt R.C. despatched to Rouen for passage to England and discharge	
	26.12.15		Fine day. Brigade moved into billets vacated by 1st Brigade. Vacated billets at 11 A.M. entered new billets at 12.30 P.M. Lieut Newton proceeded on sent leave to England 26.12.15 to 30.12.15	
	27.12.15		Fine day. Captain Wilson proceeded on leave to England 27.12.15 to 31.12.15. Sgt Judas. Cpl S.S. Bullock Cpl Sad. Jackson Cpl Sendall. Gnr Coe. Gnr Watkinson proceeded on leave to England 27.12.15 to 31.12.15. Lieut Greig relieved Brigade M.O	
	28.12.15		Fine morning. Capt Hannah RAMC "T" proceeded on sent leave 28.12.15 to 2.1.16 Lieut G.D. Wilson to be temporary Captain with effect from 16.10.15 (Auth) (T.F.3) 9/Artillery/9334 W.O. d/-18.12.15	
	29.12.15		Fine morning. Exchanged 2 H.D. Curries for 2 L.D. Curries at remounts Gonnehem. The 2 L.D Ranched over to 1st Battey. Lieut Col Crolonies leave extended to see medical board (Auth W.O)	

Army Form C. 2118

WAR DIARY
or
INTELLIGENCE SUMMARY
(Erase heading not required.)

Instructions regarding War Diaries and Intelligence Summaries are contained in F. S. Regs., Part II. and the Staff Manual respectively. Title Pages will be prepared in manuscript.

Place	Date	Hour	Summary of Events and Information	Remarks and references to Appendices
In the field	30.12.15		Fair day	
	31.12.15		Fine morning turned wet later. Sgt Wesley Smith, Cpl Broughton, Bdr Stevenson, Jepson and Till, Gnr Foster proceeded on leave to England 31.12.15 to 4.1.16. Lieut H.L. Newton returned from leave.	

Brury Lunes
Major
Lieut. Col., R.F.A., "T."
Commanding 1/4th North Midland (Howitzer) Brigade, R.F.A. "T."

1/4 N.M. Bde R.F.A.
Jan 1916
Vol XLI

Army Form C. 2118

WAR DIARY
or
INTELLIGENCE SUMMARY
(Erase heading not required.)

Instructions regarding War Diaries and Intelligence Summaries are contained in F.S. Regs., Part II. and the Staff Manual respectively. Title Pages will be prepared in manuscript.

Place	Date	Hour	Summary of Events and Information	Remarks and references to Appendices
In the field	1.1.16		Fair morning. Lieut N.R.B Eddowes proceeded on short leave to England 1.1.16 to 5.1.16. Captain G.D Wilson returned from leave. Distinguished Service in the field. Mentioned in despatches Maj W.D Drury-Lowe. Maj F.G. Crompton. B.S.M. G.Cook. Bdr.s H.Dobson. A.Robinson. Gnr. S Taylor.	
	2.1.16		Fair morning, turned wet later	
	3.1.16		Fine day. Captain Hannah R.A.M.C returned from leave	
	4.1.16		Fine day. Rdn Wagg, Webster, Arthur Garratt, Jackson, Edwards, Wear Bailey proceeded on short leave to England 4.1.16 to 8.1.16	
	5.1.16		Fine day Bdr drew 1 charger and 4 L.D. horses from remounts Gnr Oday returned from one months leave	
	6.1.16		Fine but dull day. Lieut Proper proceeded on short leave to England 6.1.16 to 10.1.16	
	7.1.16		Fine day. Received orders for brigade to entrain all vehicles and about 150 all ranks on 9th inst. Wired to Lieut Proper to rejoin at once also to men on one months leave to rejoin at once if they intended to move with their brigade.	

1875 Wt. W593/826 1,000,000 4/15 J.B.C. & A. A.D.S.S./Forms/C. 2118.

Army Form C. 2118

WAR DIARY
or
INTELLIGENCE SUMMARY

(Erase heading not required.)

Instructions regarding War Diaries and Intelligence Summaries are contained in F. S. Regs., Part II. and the Staff Manual respectively. Title Pages will be prepared in manuscript.

Place	Date	Hour	Summary of Events and Information	Remarks and references to Appendices
In the field	8.1.16		Fine day. Lieut Dufton rejoined the brigade and was attached to 1st Batty. Received orders that brigade is to entrain at Hillers Station at 6.51 A.M. on 9th inst. Gnr Kay joined the brigade from 3rd brigade R.F.A.T. Dr Herd (or Dufton's servant) rejoined brigade and attached to 1st Batty. 1 Officer 12 other ranks were attached to the brigade from the 31st Amn. Col.	
	9.1.16		Advanced portion of Brigade arrived at Hillers 6.50 A.M. Commenced entraining at 7.18 A.M. All entrained 8.51 A.M. Train departed Hillers 9.54 A.M. Train arrived Abbeville 4 P.M. Wft Abbeville 4.50 P.M.	Lieut Porter returned off leave
	10.1.16		Train arrived Montreau 6.10 A.M. Wft Montreau 6.55 A.M. Train arrived Macon 9.5 P.M. Wft Macon 10.50 P.M.	
	11.1.16		Fine morning. Train arrived Pierre-latte 6.45 A.M. Train Wft Pierre-latte 7.50 A.M. Train arrived Marseilles 1.56 P.M. Commenced detraining 2.10 P.M. Finished detraining 3.30 P.M. Reached camp La Valentine 5.45 P.M. Captain Nicol joined Brigade posted to Ammn col. Cpl Orchard + Gnr Weally returned off one months leave	

Army Form C. 2118

WAR DIARY
or
INTELLIGENCE SUMMARY
(Erase heading not required.)

Instructions regarding War Diaries and Intelligence Summaries are contained in F. S. Regs., Part II. and the Staff Manual respectively. Title Pages will be prepared in manuscript.

Place	Date	Hour	Summary of Events and Information	Remarks and references to Appendices
In the field	12.1.16		Fine day. 66 Crews & 2nd Battery entrained at Killens Station. Departed Killens 3.45 P.M. (1st Train)	
	13.1.16		Fine day. 1st train arrived Villeneuve 9 A.M. water and feed departed 9.45 A.M. arrived Montreaux 1.30 P.M. water and feed departed 2.30 P.M. 2nd train Amm. Col. entrained at Burguette Station at 1.30 P.M. finished entraining 3 P.M. departed 4.30 P.M. 3rd train which consisted of HeadQuarters 1st Battery and remainder of 2nd Battery entrained at Burguette and departed at 7.41 P.M. 2nd train arrived Etreville 11.45 P.M. water + feed departed 12.45 A.M. 14th	
	14.1.16		Fine day. Received orders about arrival of rear portion of Brigade and Horses, on evening of 15th inst. 1st train at Lyons at 8.30 A.M. water feed + breakfast departed 9.30 A.M. 2nd train arrived Villeneuve St-Georges 8 A.M. water feed breakfast departed 8.45 A.M. 3rd train arrived Villeneuve St Georges 12 BDP.M. water feed + dinner 1.20 departed 5 P.M. arrived Montreaux at 4.20 P.M. water feed departed at 5.10 P.M.	
	15.1.16		Fine day. 1st train arrived Marseilles 10.30 P.M. arrived Valentin Camp 2 A.M. 16th 2nd train arrived Paray-le-Monial at 6 A.M. water feed breakfast departed 6.45 A.M. arrived Givors noon watered Crews. Arrived le Teil 5 P.M. water feed tea departed 3rd train arrived Pierrelatte 9.15 A.M. arrived at Macon at 8 A.M. water feed + breakfast departed. 9.15 A.M. Arrived Pierrelatte 10.20 P.M. water feed departed 11.5 P.M.	

Army Form C. 2118

WAR DIARY
or
INTELLIGENCE SUMMARY
(Erase heading not required.)

Instructions regarding War Diaries and Intelligence Summaries are contained in F. S. Regs., Part II. and the Staff Manual respectively. Title Pages will be prepared in manuscript.

Place	Date	Hour	Summary of Events and Information	Remarks and references to Appendices
In the field	16.1.16		2nd Train arrived at Marseilles at 3 A.M. water + feed arrived camp Valentin 9 A.M. 3rd Train arrived Marseilles 6.30 A.M. water + feed arrived camp Valentin 10 A.M. nine reinforcements joined Brigade. Lieut Heaton thrown from his horse admitted to Hospital	
	17.1.16		Fine day. eight reinforcements joined Brigade from 46th D.A. Parks. Lieut W.K.S. Hoslem rejoined Brigade after completing duties of advance billeting officer	
	18.1.16		Fine day	
	19.1.16		Fine day. Cpls Cooper, Booth, Gnr Bratby and Dr Prime struck off strength of Brigade.	
	20.1.16		Fine day Six men dispatched to Rouen to join D.A.C	
	21.1.16		Fine day	
	22.1.16		Fine day	

Army Form C. 2118

WAR DIARY
or
INTELLIGENCE SUMMARY
(Erase heading not required.)

Instructions regarding War Diaries and Intelligence Summaries are contained in F. S. Regs., Part II. and the Staff Manual respectively. Title Pages will be prepared in manuscript.

Place	Date	Hour	Summary of Events and Information	Remarks and references to Appendices
In the field	23.1.16		Fine day.	
	24.1.16		Fine day.	
	25.1.16		Fine day.	
	26.1.16		Fine day. Major F. G. Crompton left for seven days sick leave to England. Received orders at 4-30 p.m. that Brigade would entrain on the morning of the 27th inst. Bde Hdqrs, 1st battery and all vehicles B Am: Col. would leave at 1-12 a.m. 2nd Battery complete and personnel and horses of Am: Col. would leave at 7-36 a.m. Bde Hd qrs, 1st Battery and all the vehicles B Am: Col. left La Valentine Camp at 9-10 p.m. and arrived Avenue Station (Graveilles) at 11-30 p.m.	
	27.1.16		Above portion of Bde commenced to entrain at 12-5 a.m. and finished entraining at 1-20 a.m. 1st Train left Graveilles at 2-10 a.m. arrived Orange 8-50 a.m. Horses watered and fed. Train left Orange 9-40 a.m. Train arrived Hureon 8-30 p.m. Horses watered and fed. Left Hureon 9-30 p.m. Remaining portion of Bde (2nd Battery complete and personnel & horses of Am: Col.) left La Valentine Camp at 1 A.M. 2nd Train left Graveilles at 8-45 a.m. arrived Orange at 3-30 p.m. Horses watered & fed. Train left Orange at 4-10 p.m.	

WAR DIARY or INTELLIGENCE SUMMARY

Army Form C. 2118

(Erase heading not required.)

Instructions regarding War Diaries and Intelligence Summaries are contained in F.S. Regs., Part II. and the Staff Manual respectively. Title Pages will be prepared in manuscript.

Place	Date	Hour	Summary of Events and Information	Remarks and references to Appendices
In the Field	28.1.16		2nd Train arrived Mouen at 2 a.m. Horses watered and fed. Left Mouen at 3-10 a.m. 1st train arrived Is-Sur-Tille at 7-30 a.m. Horses watered and fed. Left Is-Sur-Tille at 8-35 a.m. 2nd Train arrived Montierean at 6-10 p.m. Horses watered and fed. Left Montierean at 7-5 p.m. 1st Train arrived Nogent-Sur-Seine 6-40 p.m. Horses watered and fed. Left Nogent-Sur-Seine 7-40 p.m. 2nd Train had a slight mishap at Juvisy, where train slipped the points and collided with another train, delayed 9-50 to 10-25 p.m. Saddler Rooms 2nd Battn fell out of the train in tunnel near Dijon.	
	29.1.16		1st Train arrived Orung-Villens at 3-5 a.m. Left Orung-Villens at 2-45 a.m. 1st Train arrived Pont-Remy at 8-15 a.m., commenced to detrain 9-50 a.m., finished detraining 11 a.m. 2nd Train arrived Pont Remy at 10-30 a.m. the Bell reached Gillett at Bouchon at varous times between 2 and 4 p.m. One horse truck left behind at Amiens owing to chegerin influence arrived 8 P.M.	
	30.1.16		Dull day. One Officer 12 other ranks returned to Div. Am. Col.	

Army Form C. 2118

WAR DIARY
or
INTELLIGENCE SUMMARY
(Erase heading not required.)

Instructions regarding War Diaries and Intelligence Summaries are contained in F. S. Regs., Part II. and the Staff Manual respectively. Title Pages will be prepared in manuscript.

Place	Date	Hour	Summary of Events and Information	Remarks and references to Appendices
In field	31.1.16		Cold raw day —	

Lieut. Col., R.F.A., "T"
Commanding 1/4th North Midland (Howitzer) Brigade, R.F.A. "T."

CONFIDENTIAL.

WAR DIARY.

4th: NORTH MIDLAND BRIGADE, R.F.A.

FEBRUARY 1st: - 29th: 1916.

Vol XIII

1/1st North Midland (Staffordshire) Brigade, R.F.A.

CONFIDENTIAL

WAR DIARY.

from 1st February 1916 to 29th February 1916.

W. J. Webb
Major
Lieut-Col., R.F.A., "T.F."
Commanding 1/1th North Midland (Howitzer) Brigade, R.F.A. "T.F."

Army Form C. 2118

WAR DIARY
or
INTELLIGENCE SUMMARY
(Erase heading not required.)

Instructions regarding War Diaries and Intelligence Summaries are contained in F.S. Regs., Part II. and the Staff Manual respectively. Title Pages will be prepared in manuscript.

Place	Date	Hour	Summary of Events and Information	Remarks and references to Appendices
In the field	1.2.16		Fine cold day. Cpl Evans G.L. and Dr Moore.A. (2nd Batty) and Gnr Shaw.H. (1st Batty) despatched to Base for passage to England and discharge on expiration of engagement. Gnr Hutchings H.W. joined Brigade from 1st Brigade. Posted to 1st Batty. Lieut J.M. Spencer granted 48 hours Special leave to Paris	F.M.J
	2.2.16		Fine day.	F.M.J
	3.2.16		Fine day	F.M.J
	4.2.16		Fine day. Lieut J.M. Spencer returned from leave. B.Q.M.S. S. Spencer struck off Strength from 4.1.16 (munition work in England)	F.M.J
	5.2.16		Fine day	F.M.J

WAR DIARY
or
INTELLIGENCE SUMMARY
(Erase heading not required.)

Army Form C. 2118

Instructions regarding War Diaries and Intelligence Summaries are contained in F.S. Regs., Part II. and the Staff Manual respectively. Title Pages will be prepared in manuscript.

Place	Date	Hour	Summary of Events and Information	Remarks and references to Appendices
In the field	6.2.16		Fine day. Major F. G. Crompton returned off leave. 2/Lieut Ward sent to hospital	F.M.J
	7.2.16		Fine day. Bdr Clarkman T. Strack off strength from 27.1.16 (Transferred to England)	F.M.J
	8.2.16		Some rain. 2/Lt GIBLIN, Cpl SMITH and Cmr HILL proceeded to VAL HEUREUX on trench mortar course	F.M.J
	9.2.16		Snow during night and showers during day. The Brigade was selected for attachment to 55th DIVARTY. Lieut Col. DRURY-LOWE received orders to report to 55th DIVARTY at DOMART. 2/Lieut W. COOKE (interpreter) joined Brigade	F.M.J
	10.2.16		Fine, wet day. Lieut Col DRURY-LOWE proceeded to 55th DIVARTY, and from there proceeded to BEAUMETZ to meet Commandant MARET-MANGE of 88th French Division to reconnoitre gun positions. Returned to BOUCHON 7 P.M. Sgt CRANE attached 46th Division Signals for wireless course.	F.M.J

Army Form C. 2118

WAR DIARY
or
INTELLIGENCE SUMMARY
(Erase heading not required.)

Place	Date	Hour	Summary of Events and Information	Remarks and references to Appendices
In the field	10.2.16		Received operation order No 2 and unit of march	
	11.2.16		Very wet morning. Gnr WOOLLEY proceeded on leave to ENGLAND via HARVRE 11.1.16 to 19.1.16. Brigade and Battery commanders proceeded to reconnoitre gun positions. Lieut J.M. SPURRIER proceeded to LONGVILLERS to reconnoitre billets for the Brigade	F. MJ
	12.2.16		Wet morning, fine later. The Brigade left BOUCHON 9 A.M. and marched via DOMART-EN-PONTHIEU and FRANSU to LONGVILLERS arriving there at 1 P.M. Billetted there for the night. Lieut J.M. SPURRIER and billetting party proceeded to THIEVRES to reconnoitre billets. Lieut H.R. BEDDOWES and Cpl MANNING left behind at BOUCHON to attend gunnery course at HAVERNAS on 13th inst. Cpl HEMINGWAY left behind at BOUCHON under orders of an officer of 4th Div Amm Col to hand over billets to incoming units. Received W.O. authority for promotion of Major W.D DRURY-LOWE to Temp Lieut Col authority W.O. letter (T.F.3) 9/Artillery/390. d/29-1-16.	FMJ

Army Form C. 2118

WAR DIARY
or
INTELLIGENCE SUMMARY
(Erase heading not required.)

Instructions regarding War Diaries and Intelligence Summaries are contained in F. S. Regs., Part II. and the Staff Manual respectively. Title Pages will be prepared in manuscript.

Place	Date	Hour	Summary of Events and Information	Remarks and references to Appendices
In the field	13.2.16		Wet morning, fine later. Brigade marched to THIEVRES from LONGVILLERS via BERNAVILLE, HEM, DOULLENS, ORVILLE, Wgt Biewis Q.A.M. feed and watered horses at HEM at 12.15 P.M. to 1.15 P.M. Arrived THIEVRES 4 P.M. Lieut EDDOWES and Cpl MANNING proceeded on an artillery course at HAVERNAS from 13th to 25th. Lieut A.F. DUFTON remained behind sick.	S.W.
	14.2.16		Very showery. Brigade marched to HUMBERCOURT from THIEVRES via HALLOY and POMMERA. Left THIEVRES 8.30 A.M. arrived HUMBERCOURT 12.30 P.M. Lieut T.H.N CATTLE proceeded to BEAUMETZ to see Lieut PARKINSON 2/1st West Lancs Field Co R.E. in regard to construction of new gun emplacements. Lieut A.F. DUFTON rejoined	F.W.F.
	15.2.16		Very wet day. Battery commanders and working parties proceeded to new gun positions. Brigade commander proceeded to reconnoitre for new Brigade Head Quarters.	F.W.F.

1875 Wt. W593/826 1,000,000 4/15 J.B.C. & A. A.D.S.S./Forms/C. 2118.

WAR DIARY
or
INTELLIGENCE SUMMARY
(Erase heading not required.)

Army Form C. 2118

Place	Date	Hour	Summary of Events and Information	Remarks and references to Appendices
In the field	16.2.16		Very wet day. Brigade marched from HUMBERCOURT via GOUY-EN-ARTOIS to wagon lines at MONCHIET. Left HUMBERCOURT 9.50 A.M. arriving MONCHIET 1.30 P.M. Brigade Head Quarters established at BEAUMETZ. Working parties preparing gun positions. Ammunition column proceeded to Bivis at WARLUZEL arriving there 11 A.M.	F.M.J
	17.2.16		Fine day. Working parties preparing gun positions. 2/Lieuts PARKER and EBERY (3/3rd N.M. Brigade RFA) attached to 1st and 2nd Batterys respectively for instruction.	F.M.J
	18.2.16		Wet morning. Working parties preparing gun positions	F.M.J
	19.2.16		Wet day. Guns went into position. 1st Battery guns in position at 7.25 P.M. 2nd Battery at 8.25 P.M. 1st Battery position R9b 5.5. 2nd Battery position R9a 9.3 Sheet 51c S.E. FRANCE 1/20,000	F.M.J
	20.2.16		Fine day. Guns started registering. 1st Battery registered Mill R35a.4.4. and Sap F, R24c.7.3. 2nd Battery registered Mill R35a.4.4. and Communication Trench R 3.4 to 10.5. map references taken from Sheet 51c S.E. FRANCE 1/20,000	F.M.J
	21.2.16		Fine day. Very cold. 1st Battery registered Sap D, M19d 5.9. and Sap G, M19c 8.0. also fired 11 rounds at Sap F in retaliation. 2nd Battery registered German front line trench	F.M.J

WAR DIARY
or
INTELLIGENCE SUMMARY
(Erase heading not required.)

Army Form C. 2118

Instructions regarding War Diaries and Intelligence Summaries are contained in F. S. Regs., Part II. and the Staff Manual respectively. Title Pages will be prepared in manuscript.

Place	Date	Hour	Summary of Events and Information	Remarks and references to Appendices
In the field	21.2.16 continued		Opposite F.4 and front line trench opposite F.1 also fired 6 rounds at Mill and 8 rounds at trench opposite F.4 in retaliation. 1st Batty fired on Saps D, F, G + G.1 but with unsatisfactory results owing to faulty delineation of sures. 2nd Batty fired 30 rounds on enemy first line trenches in front of F4 obtaining range and line for all guns but delineation poor.	F.M.I
	22.2.16		Snow. 2nd Batty fired 5 rounds on enemy first line opposite F1 centre ranging one gun. Proposed munition workers were interviewed by munitions officer at 164th Brigade Head Quarters at SAULTY.	F.M.I
	23.2.16		Cold, more snow. 1st Batty fired 25 rounds at Sap Quad G's Hill, and FICHEUX crossroads, delineation of sures bad. 2/Lieut ARKWRIGHT joined Brigade posted to 2nd Batty. 2/Lieut COOKE proceeded on leave to ENGLAND 24/2/16 to 2/3/16. Cpl HEMINGWAY rejoined.	F.M.I
	24.2.16		Fine cold day. 1st Batty fired on Saps H and I registering same. 2nd Batty fired on first line trench to right of F.1. line and range obtained for all guns delineation bad. a/Bdr Hardy proceeded on leave to ENGLAND. 25/2/16 to 3/3/16.	F.M.I
	25.2.16		Very cold, more snow. 1st Batty fired 10 rounds at Sap 14.N.20.a.5.9. Ammn Col moved from WARLUZEL to SAULTY. Lieut WARLUZEL to SAULTY. 1.0PM arrived SAULTY 3.30 P.M.	F.M.I

Army Form C. 2118.

WAR DIARY
or
INTELLIGENCE SUMMARY
(Erase heading not required.)

Instructions regarding War Diaries and Intelligence Summaries are contained in F. S. Regs., Part II. and the Staff Manual respectively. Title Pages will be prepared in manuscript.

Place	Date	Hour	Summary of Events and Information	Remarks and references to Appendices
In the field	26.2.16		Fine day, thaw. 1st Batty fired 12 rounds on S of G Band D rounds unsatisfactory observation poor. 2/Lieut J.B. PROPER and C/L ELLIS proceeded for HAVERNAS to attend gunnery course. 2nd Batty registered R.29.b.7.2. observation very poor.	F.M.J
	27.2.16		Fine day. Lieut Col DRURY-LOWE proceeded to BEAUVAL to attend Senior officers artillery course. 1st Batty fired 22 rounds on S of H (M.19.d.7.9) and S of G (M.20.a.1.3) to register, but observation poor. 2nd Batty fired 25 rounds at earthwork opposite F3 doing damage and ran to work and wire. Major F.G. CROMPTON assumed temporary command of the Brigade. Lieut A.F. DUFTON attached to 46th DIV ARTY	F.M.J.
	28.2.16		cold wet day. Lieut A.F. DUFTON rejoined Brigade. 2nd Batty fired 23 rounds to check target lines and register.	F.M.J
	29.2.16		Fine morning wet afternoon. 2nd Batty fired 6 rounds to check registration	F.M.J

N Crawly
Major
Lieut. Col. R.F.A.
Commanding 1/2th North Midland (Howitzer) Brigade R.F.A.

CONFIDENTIAL

WAR DIARY.

4th: NORTH MIDLAND BRIGADE. R.F.A.

March 1st: to 31st: 1916.

CONFIDENTIAL.

1/4th North Mid. (How.) Brigade. R.F.A.

WAR DIARY.

for

MARCH 1916.

[signed] Picot McAdie
Lieut. Col., R.F.A., "T."
Commanding 1/4th North Midland (Howitzer) Brigade, R.F.A. "T."

Army Form C. 2118

WAR DIARY
or
INTELLIGENCE SUMMARY
(Erase heading not required.)

Instructions regarding War Diaries and Intelligence Summaries are contained in F.S. Regs., Part II. and the Staff Manual respectively. Title Pages will be prepared in manuscript.

Place	Date	Hour	Summary of Events and Information	Remarks and references to Appendices
In the field	1.3.16		Fine day warmer. 1st Batty fired 8 rounds at Sap H (M.19.d 7.9.) to register. 2nd Batty fired 20 rounds at R.29.c.7.1. resulting in damage to enemy's works and 8 rounds at X roads X 4.a 8:7.	F.M.I.
	2.3.16		Fine day. 3 Officers and 13 other ranks of "A" Battery 154th Brigade R.F.A attached to Brigade for instruction. 1st Batty fired 17 rounds at Sap H (M 19 d. 7.9.) with satisfactory results. 2nd Batty fired 14 rounds at trench opposite F3 and F4 also at 3.30 P.M. fired 14 rounds at communication trench between R 25 a. 0.6. and R 35 a. 1/2. 4. 2nd Batty fired 9 rounds shrapnel with good effect.	F.M.I
	3.3.16		Dull day. Some rain. 1st Batty fired 23 rounds at Sap F (R 24 c 8.3) to register also at 7 P.M. and 7.5. P.M. fired Salvos at LE CHAT MAIGRE (M 27 a 6 1/2. 8) by order of C.R.A. 2nd Batty fired 7 rounds at 1st line trench in front of F1 right and 19 rounds at communication trench and support trenches on the right of FICHEUX Mill. Lieut Col W.D DRURY-LOWE rejoined Brigade.	F.M.I
	4.3.16		Snow all day. Lieut Col W.D DRURY-LOWE proceeded to Head Quarters 34th French Division at HAUTE-AVENES to reconnoitre gun positions. 2/Lieut COOK returned from leave	

Army Form C. 2118

WAR DIARY
or
INTELLIGENCE SUMMARY
(Erase heading not required.)

Place	Date	Hour	Summary of Events and Information	Remarks and references to Appendices
In the field	5.3.16		Fine bright day. 3 Officers and 13 other ranks of "A" Batty 154th Brigade RFA returned to their own unit on completion of attachment. 1st Batty fired 15 rounds Shrapnel at S of H (M19 d T.9) with satisfactory results. 2nd Batty fired 20 rounds at Communication Trench east of BLAIRVILLE WOOD and BLAIRVILLE WOOD. Left Section of 1st Batty relieved by a Section of B/85th Batty at 11.22 P.M. Right Section of 2nd Batty relieved by a Section of B/85th Batty at 11.25 P.M. Both Sections marched to Wagon lines at MONCHIET.	F.M.J
	6.3.16		Bright day. Remaining Sections of both batteries withdrawn at 7.30 P.M. and marched to Wagon lines at MONCHIET.	F.M.J
	7.3.16		Brigade marched from MONCHIET to GOUY-EN-TERNOIS VIA SIMENCOURT, WANQUETIN, LATTRE-ST QUENTIN, AVESNES-LE-CONTE and PENIN, leaving MONCHIET 9.10 A.M. and arriving GOUY-EN-TERNOIS 3.30 P.M. Captain NEWTON and Lieut CATTLE proceeded to gun positions to reconnoitre and remain there till the batteries come into action. Lieut EDDOWES rejoined Brigade from gunnery course. Received orders that "A/154th Batty and Section Amm col would proceed to CAUCORT and 2nd Batty and Section of Amm col would proceed to ACQ both on 8.3.16	F.M.J

Army Form C. 2118

WAR DIARY
or
INTELLIGENCE SUMMARY
(Erase heading not required.)

Instructions regarding War Diaries and Intelligence Summaries are contained in F.S. Regs., Part II. and the Staff Manual respectively. Title Pages will be prepared in manuscript.

Place	Date	Hour	Summary of Events and Information	Remarks and references to Appendices
In the field	8.3.16		Fine day. "A"/154 Batty and Section Amm col proceeded to CAUCORT under orders of LEFT GROUP Commander. 2nd Batty and Section Amm col proceeded to ACQ under orders of CENTRE GROUP Commander. Major CROMPTON and Captain NICOL proceeded to reconnoitre at gun positions. N° 362 Sgt MANNING reported after gunnery course. Cpl CROFTS, Bdrs BOOTH and COOPER and Gnr BRATBY joined Brigade from Base. Received instructions to the effect that the future nomenclature of A/154 Batty will be "R" Batty 1/4 N.M. (How) Bde R.F.A.T. (formerly A.G.G.H.Q. D/1242 d/3.3.16 "R" Batty departed GOUY-EN-ARTOIS. 8.30 A.M. arriving CAUCORT 1.0 P.M. R Batty had two guns in action at 10.30 P.M. 2nd Batty departed GOUY-EN-ARTOIS at 8.30 A.M. arriving ACQ 3.0 P.M. 2nd guns of 2nd Batty in action at 11. P.M. "R" Batty position x 22 b 6.9. (Sheet 36 b 1/40000) 2nd Batty position S 25 d 5.8. (Sheet 36 C 1/40000)	F.W.I.
	9.3.16		Fine day. Bdr EVANS a/Bdr GUDGER, Gnr ILLSLEY, Gnr MARTIN, Gnr STONE, Gnr SWAIN, Dr GRIMES and Dr HEARNDEN proceeded to VALHEUREUX for trench mortar course at 3rd ARMY SCHOOL. 2/Lieut COOKE and Servant attached to 46th Div ARTY as LIAISON OFFICER. Left Section 2nd Batty left ACQ and joined right Section in action both guns in position 1.30 A.M. on 10th 2nd Batty regained the GLASS HOUSE firing 19 rounds.	F.W.I.
	10.3.16		Misty day. Remaining Section of "R" Battery went into action both guns in position at 9.15 P.M. 1st Batty and remaining Section of Amm col marched to VILLERS-CHATEL leaving GOUY-EN-TERNOIS at 10.30 A.M. under orders of O.C. 1st Bde R.F.A.T. arriving VILLERS CHATEL 4.0 P.M 2/Lieut PROPER and Cpl ELLIS returned from gunnery School at 3rd ARMY SCHOOL.	F.M.I.

1875. Wt. W593/826 1,000,000 4/15 J.B.C. & A. A.D.S.S./Forms/C. 2118.

Army Form C. 2118

WAR DIARY
or
INTELLIGENCE SUMMARY
(Erase heading not required.)

Instructions regarding War Diaries and Intelligence Summaries are contained in F.S. Regs., Part II. and the Staff Manual respectively. Title Pages will be prepared in manuscript.

Place	Date	Hour	Summary of Events and Information	Remarks and references to Appendices
In the field	11.3.16		Dull day some rain, Brigade Head Quarters marched from GOUY-EN-TERNOIS at 10 A.M. to ECOIVRES arriving 4 P.M. 1st Batty marched from VILLERS-CHATEL at 1.30 P.M. to ACQ arriving thus 3.30 P.M. at 7 P.M. one section 1st Batty went into action at F.18.c.2.9. (Sheet 51C) Lieut Col L.G GISBORNE rejoined Brigade from ENGLAND. Lieut WK'S HASLAM proceeded to MOUNT KEMMEL to attend Sound ranging course. 2nd Batty wagon lines moved from ACQ to CAMBLAIN L'ABBE arriving in billets at 3.30 P.M. 2nd Batty retaliated on GLASS HOUSE, TRANCHEE-DE-LA-HAIE.	F.W.3
	12.3.16		Fine day. Lieut Col GISBORNE assumed command of the Brigade. 1st Batty registered cross roads at A11 a.9.9. and crater S28 d.5.8. (Sheet 36c S.W.) 2nd Batty registered COMMAN'S EARTH WORK on left of GLASS HOUSE, POTSDAM at K 4, TRENCHEE DU CHATEAU "R" Batty fired 13 rounds at 5.15 b.1.5. and 30 rounds at LA FOLIE CHATEAU, S.23c.1.3	F.W.3
	13.3.16		Fine day Brigade Head Quarters moved forward to BERTHONVAL FARM. Lieut Col DRURY-LOWE posted to 2nd Batty. 1st Batty registered following points:- A 4 d.7.2., A 4 d.7.6, A 4 d 5½.9 and A 5 d.1½.5 (Sheet 36c S.W.)	F.W.3

WAR DIARY
or
INTELLIGENCE SUMMARY

(Erase heading not required.)

Army Form C. 2118

Place	Date	Hour	Summary of Events and Information	Remarks and references to Appendices
In the field	13.3.16 continued		2nd Batty fired 10 rounds to register BOYAU-DU-TAILLIS NORD also 16 rounds in retaliation on TRENCHEE-DE-LA HAIE and EARTHWORK. "R" Batty registered LA FOLIE CHATEAU (30 rounds) and LA FOLIE FARM (25 rounds), Remaining Section of 1st Batty went into action.	F.M.I
	14.3.16		Fine day. 1st Batty registered again the following points, cross roads A11a 9.9., craters S28 d 5.8. A4 d 7.2., A4 d 7.6, A4 d 5½.9. A5 d 11/2.5. (sheet 36c SW). 2nd Batty fired 13 rounds in retaliation at POTSDAM and the TRENCHE-DU-CHATEAU. "R" Batty registered LA FOLIE FARM S29a 4.4. and S23c 13. also fired 12 rounds at GIVENCHY S9d 9.3.	F.M.I
	16.3.16		Fine day. Head Quarters wagon lines moved from ECOIVRES to ACQ. 1st Batty registered following points. A5 d 2½.9., S29a 1.1., S29a 1.4. 2nd Batty fired several series at PETIT VIMY in retaliation. "R" Batty fired at S9c 6.4. LA FOLIE CHATEAU S23c.13 and BOYAU LA VERITE	F.M.I

WAR DIARY or INTELLIGENCE SUMMARY

Army Form C. 2118

Place	Date	Hour	Summary of Events and Information	Remarks and references to Appendices
In the field	16.3.16		Fine day. Twelve Reinforcements joined the Brigade and posted to 2nd Batty. N°393 Sgt CRANE sent to Base for passage to ENGLAND and discharge on termination of engagement. 1st Batty registered TILLEUL Village A5c9.3. 2nd Batty fired 34 rounds to register and demolish crater S.W of BOIS CARRE doing considerable damage to works. "R" Batty fired at R.3. and T. (Reg Trench Sector Map 52)	F.M.T
	17.3.16		Fine day. 2/Lieut COOKE rejoined from 46th DIV-ARTY. Lieut Col DRURY-LOWE left for ENGLAND and struck off Strength. 1st Batty registered A4 a 8.3. From 7 to 10 PM 1st Batty fired 40 rounds at cross roads South of TILLEUL Village and TILLEUL Village, A11a 9.9 and A5d 1.4. supporting minor ops from C.R.A. (Sheet 51bNW.) 2nd Batty Registered L'APPENDICE and TRENCHE-DE-LA-HAIE "R" Batty fired 5 rounds at trench de FRANK FORT and 8 rounds at LA VOLEIR	F.M.T

WAR DIARY
or
INTELLIGENCE SUMMARY
(Erase heading not required.)

Army Form C. 2118

Instructions regarding War Diaries and Intelligence Summaries are contained in F.S. Regs., Part II. and the Staff Manual respectively. Title Pages will be prepared in manuscript.

Place	Date	Hour	Summary of Events and Information	Remarks and references to Appendices
In the field	18.3.16		Fine day. The following N.C.O.s and men despatched to HAVRE for munition test. N° 353 Sgt HEMINGWAY, N° 358 Sgt BOWRING, N° 439 Br WEBSTER N° 242 Cpl GARRATT N° 541 T/Cpl ROGERS, N° 984 GREGORY, N° 1012 Gnr VICKERS. N° 820 Gnr CLEWS N° 1430 Dr FOWERS, N° 1493 Gnr GRIMES, N° 659 Gnr JEPHSON, and N° 990 Dr ARMITAGE 2nd Batty fired 3 rounds in retaliation R' Batty fired 12 rounds at cross roads South of GIVENCHY and 12 rounds at Battery positions near FOSSE 1. 2/Lieut A HEATON rejoined from England	F.M.T F.M.T
	19.3.16		Fine day, 1st Batty fired 20 rounds at BOYAU-DES-AVOCATS (31 and 32, 596 and 597) on French map N° 2 (Centre) 2nd Batty fired 2 series on BOYAU DE LA VERITE, TRENCHEE-DE LA JUSTICE and TRENCHEE DU CHATEAU R' Batty registered target South of GIVENCHY firing 20 rounds.	F.M.T

WAR DIARY
or
INTELLIGENCE SUMMARY

(Erase heading not required.)

Army Form C. 2118

Instructions regarding War Diaries and Intelligence Summaries are contained in F.S. Regs., Part II. and the Staff Manual respectively. Title Pages will be prepared in manuscript.

Place	Date	Hour	Summary of Events and Information	Remarks and references to Appendices
In the field	20.3.16		Fine day. The three sections of Amm Col concentrated in billets at ACQ. 1st Batty fired 15 rounds at TILLEUR Village and 3 rounds on enemy trenches in co-operation with infantry patrols. 2nd Batty fired in retaliation on TRENCHEE-DE-LA-HAIE doing slight damage to trench also fired on POTSDAM, GLASS HOUSE, LA FOLIE FARM, and TRENCHEE DU GARD R' Batty fired 4 rounds at LA FOLIE CHATEAU and 17 rounds at I4	F.M.5
	21.3.16		Dull day slight rain. 1st Batty fired 15 rounds at A11 a.q.q. (TILLEUL VILLAGE) in retaliation 2nd Batty fired at following targets for aggravation and retaliation. POTSDAM, GLASS HOUSE, LA FOLIE FARM, TRENCHEE-DU-GARD. TRENCHEE DE LA HAIE, EARTH WORK N.W. of LA FOLIE FARM and TRENCHEE DU CHATEAU "R" Batty fired 10 rounds at CROSS ROADS South of GIVENCHY. Green reinforcements joined Brigade 2nd Batty fired in retaliation again on TRENCHEE-DE-LA HAIE and TRENCHEE-DU-CHATEAU	F.M.5
	22.3.16		Dull. Some rain. Lieut CATTLE proceeded to ENGLAND to attend gunnery course at LARK HILL commencing on 25.3.16. Lieut Col GISBORNE assumed temporary command of RIGHT GROUP during absence of Lieut Col TONGE 1st NM Bde R.F.A.T 2nd Batty fire on TRENCHEE-DE-LA HAIE, and TRENCHE DU CHATEAU, TAILLIS NORD and POTSDAM for aggravation	F.M.5

1875 Wt. W593/826 1,000,000 4/15 J.B.C. & A. A.D.S.S./Forms/C. 2118.

Army Form C. 2118

WAR DIARY
or
INTELLIGENCE SUMMARY
(Erase heading not required.)

Instructions regarding War Diaries and Intelligence Summaries are contained in F. S. Regs., Part II. and the Staff Manual respectively. Title Pages will be prepared in manuscript.

Place	Date	Hour	Summary of Events and Information	Remarks and references to Appendices
In the field	23.3.16		Cold, Some rain. 1st Batty fired 4 rounds at TILLEUL VILLAGE A5 c 9.3. 2nd Batty fired 3 rounds on enemy EARTH WORKS N.W. of GLASS HOUSE to check the shooting of which Gd been temporarily faulty, also fired on TRENCHEE DU GARDE and TRENCHEE DU CHATEAU, also fired on BOYAU DUTAILLIS NORD, and POTSDAM "K4". R'' Batty fired 21 rounds to register French mortar position to the right of LA VOLIER. 2/Lieut PROPER, Staff Sergt F. GILBERT, B. LLOYD, and Gnr. KILSBY and LANE proceeded on short leave to ENGLAND. 24.3.16 to 31.3.16 B.QMS HEWITT, Sergt POUNTAIN and Dr BARKER H.E. (1176) proceeded to ENGLAND on one months leave 24.3.16 to 21.4.16. at 10 P.M. 1st Batty fired 10 rounds at TILLEUL VILLAGE.	F.M.J.
	24.3.16		Snow. 2nd Batty fired in retaliation POTSDAM, K4, HANOVER, O4. APPENDICE, BOYAU DE L'ESCALIE.	F.M.J.
	25.3.16		Cold, Snow showers. Cpt PACEY and Gnr KIRKLAND proceeded to N° 13 Squadron R.F.C. at SAVY for Scout drivers course. 5 reinforcements joined Brigade from Base Depot. Two posted to each Battery and one attached to H.Q. 2nd Batty fired 2 rounds on earthwork N.W. of LA FOLIE FARM to disperse enemy working party, and fired in retaliation on BOYAU DUTAILLIS NORD, TRENCHEE DE LA HAIE BOYAU-DES-COMMANS	F.M.J.

Army Form C. 2118

WAR DIARY
or
INTELLIGENCE SUMMARY

(Erase heading not required.)

Instructions regarding War Diaries and Intelligence Summaries are contained in F. S. Regs., Part II. and the Staff Manual respectively. Title Pages will be prepared in manuscript.

Place	Date	Hour	Summary of Events and Information	Remarks and references to Appendices
In the field	26.3.16		Rain all day. 2/Lieut BURRA S.H. and No 359 Sergt MANNING. T. proceeded to HAUTECLOQUE to attend gunnery course. 2nd Batty registered P3 and TRENCHES DE LA FOLIE by order of CENTRE GROUP. "R" Batty registered TRENCH MORTAR position about S15d 7.5. and also another about S15a 5.2. and Trench S16.c.5.2. 2nd Batty fired 4 rounds at road junction S30 d 3.9.	F.W.J.
	27.3.16		Cold showers. Lieut T.M. SPURRIER Bom- FLINT.G and FLINT.D. REDFERN.A. SHARRATT.E. PEARCE.T. and TAYLOR and Gnr DICKINSON proceeded on short leave to ENGLAND 28.3.16 to 4.4.16	F.W.J
	28.3.16		Sunny day. 1st Batty fired 2 series at Target 11. 2nd Batty fired on enemy working party about 31.75/597.1. 1st Batty fired 8 rounds at crater B4 (A4b 2.5.) 2nd Batty fired 6 rounds on P3	F.W.J

Army Form C. 2118

WAR DIARY
or
INTELLIGENCE SUMMARY
(Erase heading not required.)

Place	Date	Hour	Summary of Events and Information	Remarks and references to Appendices
In the field	29.3.16		Fine bright day. 1st Batty fired 36 rounds at crater B6 (A4.b.2.5) and 138 rounds at point 515 52 C.A.4.b.9.3. Sent 36c SW) and B6 and B7(M.2.8.c.9.3. Sent 51.6 NW) 2nd Batty fired on TRENCHEE-DU-SUAYE and TRENCHEE DU HANOVER for retaliation and aggression. 'R' Batty fired on two roads South of GIVENCHY, BOIS CARRÉ (S.21.a.3.2½) and LAVOLIER crater	F.M.I
	30.3.16		Fine day. 2nd Batty heavily shelled by enemy one gun out of action. Bdr REDFERN F. Gnrs STAFFORD and Dr DICKENSON wounded	F.M.I
	31.3.16		Fine day summer. Lieut Col L.G. GISBORNE assumed command of LEFT GROUP, during temporary absence of Lnt Col Sir HILL-CHILD. 1st Batty fired on the MILL, THELUS A.6.a.7.0 and T.2.(S.28.d.5.3.) 'R' Batty fired Cross roads South of GIVENCHY and machine gun emplacement snipers post resulting in considerable damage to target. Lieut T.H.N. CATTLE, Cpl Ft. YEOMANS, Bdr REDFERN. S.S. HOOSON Gnrs PEAT, ROBINSON, and HILL and Dr POYSER granted Short leave to ENGLAND 1.4.16 to 8.1.16	F.M.I

Lieut Col., R.F.A. "T"
Commanding 1/4th North Midland (Howitzer) Brigade, R.F.A. "T"

Am 46

Vol XV

CONFIDENTIAL.

1/4th North Midland (Howitzer) Brigade, R.F.A. T.

―――――

WAR DIARY

―――――

from 1st to 30th APRIL '16.

Lionel Milne
Lieut. Col., R.F.A., "p",
Commanding 1/4th North Midland (Howitzer) Brigade, R.F.A., "T".

Army Form C. 2118

WAR DIARY
or
INTELLIGENCE SUMMARY

(Erase heading not required.)

Instructions regarding War Diaries and Intelligence Summaries are contained in F. S. Regs., Part II. and the Staff Manual respectively. Title Pages will be prepared in manuscript.

Place	Date	Hour	Summary of Events and Information	Remarks and references to Appendices
In the field	1.4.16		Fine day. 1st Batty fired on the following targets to-day:- S28d 5.8.; S28d 5.3. A11d 5.8. A5a 7.4. S2a c 2.5. and A6c 7.9.	F.M.T
			2nd Batty fired 40 rounds at TRANCHEE DU L'ESCALIER and 20 rounds at machine gun emplacement in S28L 87.	
			"R" Batty fired 35 rounds to silence trench mortar.	
	2.4.16		Fine day. 1st Batty fired 121 rounds at T2 (S28d 5.3.) at request of infantry. 2nd Batty fired 17 rounds at S28d 8½.7. R Batty fired 8 rounds to silence trench mortar. 2/Lieut W.W. Jackson joined Brigade (posted to 2nd Batty)	F.M.T
	3.4.16		Fine day. 1st Batty fired at S28d 5.8. (33 rounds) and 93 rounds at S28d 5.3. 2nd Batty fired 20 rounds at TRANCHEES DU-GARDE HANOVRE, and DU CHATEAU "R" Batty fired 33 rounds at trench mortar.	F.M.T

Army Form C. 2118

WAR DIARY
or
INTELLIGENCE SUMMARY
(Erase heading not required.)

Instructions regarding War Diaries and Intelligence Summaries are contained in F. S. Regs., Part II. and the Staff Manual respectively. Title Pages will be prepared in manuscript.

Place	Date	Hour	Summary of Events and Information	Remarks and references to Appendices
In the field	4.4.16		Fine day. Cpl HARDY (R.A.M.C.), Bdr BRIGGS, Gnrs WOOLGAR, MOON and BECKETT and Drs WILSON, MATTHEWS and BARKER J. proceeded on short leave to ENGLAND 5.4.16 to 12.4.16. 1st Batty fired 202 rounds at various targets at request of infantry and in pursuance of operation order. 2nd Batty fired 50 rounds at various targets in retaliation. "R" Batty fired 5 rounds from flank gun to regain front line trench also inspected machine gun emplacement S15d 4.7. Medical Officer commenced to inoculate the Brigade.	F.M.J
	5.4.16		Fine day 1st Batty fired at S28d S.3. and A4b 3.3. at request of infantry. 2nd Batty fired in retaliation at BOYAU DU NORD and TRANCHEE DU HANOVRE. R Batty fired 12 rounds at trench mortar LAVOLIER at urgent request of infantry. Corps commander inspected Horses of Brigade	F.M.J
	6.4.16		Fine day	F.M.J
	7.4.16		Fine day 1st Batty fired 4 bounds at string works in A4d 3½.4. at request of infantry. 2nd Batty engaged TRANCHEE DU HANOVRE 2/Lieut PARKER proceeded on leave to ENGLAND 7.4.16 to 15.4.16	F.M.J

WAR DIARY or INTELLIGENCE SUMMARY

Army Form C. 2118

Instructions regarding War Diaries and Intelligence Summaries are contained in F.S. Regs., Part II. and the Staff Manual respectively. Title Pages will be prepared in manuscript.

(Erase heading not required.)

Place	Date	Hour	Summary of Events and Information	Remarks and references to Appendices
In the field	8.4.16		Fine day. Major BUXTON-SMITH, S.S. LAWRENCE Gnrs WOOLGAR, RADFORD, and BAILEY, Fr BERRESFORD and Dr RIDGWAY and FEATHERSTONE proceeded on short leave to ENGLAND 9.4.16 to 16.4.16. 2/Lieut BORRA and Sergt MANNING J returned from gunnery course at HAUTECLOQUE. Cpl PACEY returned from wireless course. 2nd Batty fired 6 rounds at junction of BOIS de L'APPENDICE and TRANCHEE-DE-LA-FOLIE also 9 rounds at crater near BOIS CAREE "R" Batty fired at S.15 d 8.4. (M.G.) LA VOLIER S.15 d 3.9. and crater at road junction S.15 d 6.4.	F.M.J.
	9.4.16		Fine day. 1st Batty fired at T.G S 28 d 5.3. (15 rounds) at infantry kamel. 2nd Batty fired 10 rounds on enemy work North of LA FOLIE FARM Lieut MacBAIN and Sergt A MOLD proceeded to HAUTECLOQUE to attend artillery course at 3rd Army School	F.M.J.
	10.4.16		Fine day 1st Batty fired 26 rounds at A 4 d 3½.4 under group orders 2nd Batty fired 9 rounds at target trough N of LA FOLIE FARM.	F.M.J.
	11.		Fine day	

Army Form C. 2118.

WAR DIARY
or
INTELLIGENCE SUMMARY
(Erase heading not required.)

Instructions regarding War Diaries and Intelligence Summaries are contained in F.S. Regs., Part II. and the Staff Manual respectively. Title Pages will be prepared in manuscript.

Place	Date	Hour	Summary of Events and Information	Remarks and references to Appendices
In the field	12.4.16		Wet day. 1st Batty fired 8 rounds at T.G. S28 d 0.3. under group orders also 13 rounds at S29 c 2.2. Int: light very poor. "R" Batty fired 10 rounds at S22 b 4.9. 2/Bom ORTON a/Bdr FROST Gnr FLICK, SMITH, WARD, and HANSON, Dr HEALEY and APPLEBY proceeded on Sent leave to ENGLAND 13th to 20th 2/Lieut WALDRON proceeded to ENGLAND to attend course at LARKHILL	F.M.T
	13.4.16		Wet day. 1st Batty engaged the following targets. A4d 3½.4, S28b 8.7. BOYAU des SAULES, A4 b 10.8. to A4 L 7.5. THELUS, A12 a 4.9. 2nd Batty fired on the following targets with HE and Schrapnel. Enemy working party W. of GLASS HOUSE EARTHWORK N.W. of LA FOLIE FARM. New strong point on TRANCHEE LECANTE K6 and P6 R Batty fired 12 rounds behind T.4 trench and 25 rounds at LAVOLIER. Men proceeding on leave 12.4.16 shined Cretion not later than 18.4.16.	F.M.T

WAR DIARY or INTELLIGENCE SUMMARY

(Erase heading not required.)

Army Form C. 2118

Place	Date	Hour	Summary of Events and Information	Remarks and references to Appendices
In the field	14.4.16		Sunny day. 1st Batty fired 20 rounds at M.G. emplacement A10b 9.9 with good results. 'R' Batty engaged the following targets S15 d.9.1. LAVOIER and S15 b 7.6. Lieut J.M. SPURRIER granted 14 days special leave (Country 17th corps 9/81) W/R Sgt SMITH T. proceeded on 1 months leave 15.4.16 to 13.5.16. Lieut Col GISBORNE rejoined Brigade.	F.M.J.
	15.4.16		Sunny day. 1st Batty fired 30 rounds at CHALK MOUNDS A4 d 4.4. with good results. 2nd Batty engaged the following targets TRANCHEE-DU-HANOVRE, TRANCHEE-DU-SUABE and Crater S22a ½.½. 'R' Batty fired on following targets, trenches about S15 d. 9.0., S22 a 3.3, I 4 (S15a 6.1.) and S15 d. 6.4. Men who proceeded on leave on 12.4.16 were stopped at BOULOGNE and rejoined this day.	F.M.J.
	16.4.16		Fine day. Lieut Col GISBORNE proceeded to attend Senior Officers Artillery course. 1st Batty fired 107 rounds at various targets in retaliation. 2nd Batty fired on following targets S17 c ½.2., S28a 9½.9, S23a 2.9, S23a 0.8, and 9 rounds at same targets under aeroplane observation.	F.M.J.

Army Form C. 2118

WAR DIARY
or
INTELLIGENCE SUMMARY

(Erase heading not required.)

Instructions regarding War Diaries and Intelligence Summaries are contained in F.S. Regs., Part II. and the Staff Manual respectively. Title Pages will be prepared in manuscript.

Place	Date	Hour	Summary of Events and Information	Remarks and references to Appendices
In the field	17.4.16		Snowy day cold. Major Buxton Smith returned from leave. 1st Batty fired 6 rounds per gun for 5 guns at A+d 5½.9. under gun fire orders 2nd Batty fired on following targets S28b 0.9., S28b 11½.5½, S28b 1.7. S22c 8.3. S22d 5.½. S22c 6½.6½. and S28b 11½.5½. Also fired 2 rounds to test efficiency of female screen	F.M.J.
	18.4.16		Wet day. 1st Batty fired 20 rounds over trench O 61 all round of infantry and 8 rounds on THELUS and 2nd Batty fired a few rounds at T B. A23 a 20.	F.M.J
	19.4.16		Wet day. Lieut E.S. HASLAM. Joined the Brigade and attached to 1st Batty. 3 O.R. joined Brigade and posted to 1st Batty. Received operation order No 49 regarding move into rest billets 1st Batty fired on following targets, A5 a 4.6., A5 a 8.S. and LANG BOYAU 2nd Batty fired 26 rounds on following targets S28 b 8½.7. S25c 11½.1½. S22 c 9.7½. S29 a 3.3. S22 a 3½.2. 'R' Batty fired on following targets S23 c 1.3. S15 d 2.6. S15 d 5.5. S15 a 2.5. and others	F M J
	20.4.16		Fair day. 1st Batty fired Shrapnell and HE on target N Gregoti 2nd Batty fired on following targets S23 a 3½.14½ S22 c 9.7½ S22 a 3½.2. S23 a 3½.4½.2. 'R' Batty fired on various targets	F.M.J

WAR DIARY
INTELLIGENCE SUMMARY

Army Form C. 2118.

Hour, Date, Place	Summary of Events and Information	Remarks and References to Appendices
In the field		
21.4.16	Fine morning and later. Heard Lt. GISBORNE rejoined Brigade. 1st Batty fired 7 rounds on dugout E of LILLE ROAD A5d 3½.9. 2nd Batty fired 10 rounds on S22d 5.6.	F.M.J.
22.4.16	Wet day. 1st Batty fired 20 rounds on LESTILLEULS VILLAGE. 2nd Batty fired on S22C 9½.7½ and S22a 3½.11½. R Batty fired at target about S15d 5.6.	F.M.J
23.4.16	Fine day. 2/Lieut BURRA proceeded to ENGLAND to attend 4th Course at LARKHILL on 26.4.16. 1st Batty fired Scrapnel and H.E. at Sap + R.E. dump at crossroads between THELUS and LESTILLEULS also on LESTILLEULS VILLAGE. 2nd Batty engaged following targets. S22a 3½.1½. S20d 4.9. T19a 1.0, S28b 7½.7. One section of each battery relieved by one section 113 Brigade batteries 9.0 P.M. to 10.30 P.M. and marched to GRAND CAMP amusing there	F.M.J

Army Form C. 2118.

WAR DIARY
or
INTELLIGENCE SUMMARY.
(Erase heading not required.)

Instructions regarding War Diaries and Intelligence Summaries are contained in F. S. Regs., Part II. and the Staff Manual respectively. Title pages will be prepared in manuscript.

Hour, Date, Place	Summary of Events and Information	Remarks and References to Appendices
In the field		
24.4.16	Fine day. 2nd Batty fired on S30d 3.7. T19c 2.8½. S22a 3.2. and S28b 8½.7. "R" Batty fired at LA VOLIERE S15d 5.6. to Silesia trench mortar	F.M.J
25.4.16	Fine day. 2nd Batty engaged target at T19c 1½.9. "R" Batty fired on the CHATEAU. Bm̄rs ORTON and FROST, Gn̄rs SMITH, WARD & HARRISON and Drs HEALY and APPLEBY proceeded on Gnl leave to ENGLAND 26.4.16 to 3.5.16. Remaining Sections of our Batteries relieved by remaining Sections of 113th Bde Batteries and between 8.20 P.M. and 9.5 P.M. and marched to GRAND CAMP. Amn Col, and marched to GRAND CAMP. Bde H.Q. relieved by 113th Bde H.Q and marched to GRAND CAMP	F.M.J

WAR DIARY
or
INTELLIGENCE SUMMARY.
(Erase heading not required.)

Army Form C. 2118.

Hour, Date, Place	Summary of Events and Information	Remarks and references to Appendices
In the field 26.4.16	Fine day. Brigade arrived in camp at GRAND CAMP. Bdr FLINT D, Bdr ARCHER A. and Bdr RIPLEY proceeded to Anti gas School AGNIERES for course.	F.M.J
27.4.16	Fine day	F.M.J
28.4.16	Fine day. Bdr ROBINSON, Proceeded to 46 Div Signal to for course in repairs of instruments and telephony. Brig Gen R.A. 46 Division inspected the Brigade in drill order dismounted.	F.M.J
29.4.16	Fine day. Gnrs WEBB, DURANT and Bdr NOBLE proceeded to ROELLECOURT to attend divisional Signalling course. Gnr MARSHALL proceeded to DUISSANS to attend course in identification of aircraft	F.M.J

Army Form C. 2118.

WAR DIARY
or
INTELLIGENCE SUMMARY.
(Erase heading not required.)

Hour, Date, Place	Summary of Events and Information	Remarks and References to Appendices
In the field		
29.4.16 (cont)	Lt Joyce, 2r Spencer, 2r Garratt, 2r Hancock, 2r Pegg & 2r Morton to Lester, Sherwood proceeded on short leave to England from 30.4.16. to 7.5.16.	MRRB
30/4/16	Lt MRRB. Erskine took up the duties of Adjutant during Lt Joyce's absence. Fine day	MRRB

Purcell Taylor
Lieut. Col., R.F.A., "T"

CONFIDENTIAL

WAR DIARY.

233rd: BRIGADE. R.F.A.

late 1/4 NM Bde

May 1st: to 31st: 1916.

CONFIDENTIAL.

233RD BRIGADE R.F.A.

War Diary

for the month of

MAY 1916.

[signature]
LIEUT.-COL. R.F.A.
COMDG. 233RD BRIGADE, R.F.A.

Army Form C. 2118.

WAR DIARY
~~INTELLIGENCE SUMMARY~~
(Erase heading not required.)

Instructions regarding War Diaries and Intelligence Summaries are contained in F. S. Regs., Part II. and the Staff Manual respectively. Title pages will be prepared in manuscript.

Hour, Date, Place	Summary of Events and Information	Remarks and References to Appendices
In the Field 1/5/16	Fine day.	W.R.B.
2/5/16	Slowery Captain A.P. Nichol has proceeded to ENGLAND to attend course at LARKHILL. Fatigue Parties under Lt. Dufton & Lt. Proper rejoined the Brigade. Lt. J.M. Spurrier granted extension of sick leave.	W.R.B.
3/5/16	Lieut S.H. Burra granted 7 days leave to England. 2/Lts Martin, Lord, Longdon, Hegg, Raines & Fetch. W's Featherdicey granted short leave to England from 4/5/16 to 11/5/16. Fine day.	W.R.B.
4/5/16	Fine day. Colonel Gisborne & Captain Newton left here on a reconnaissance prior to our moving into new area at	W.R.B.

WAR DIARY
or
INTELLIGENCE SUMMARY.
(Erase heading not required.)

Army Form C. 2118.

Instructions regarding War Diaries and Intelligence Summaries are contained in F. S. Regs., Part II. and the Staff Manual respectively. Title pages will be prepared in manuscript.

Hour, Date, Place	Summary of Events and Information	Remarks and References to Appendices
In the field 5/5/16	Fine day. Br. Robinson rejoined Brigade after attachment to the Divisional Signal Company for course in repair of instruments. Br. Nobes & Dpr Durrant Webb rejoined Brigade after signalling course	
6/5/16	Fine day. 2nd Derby Battery marched to BERLENCOURT, leaving GRAND CAMP at 11.30 A.M. and arriving BERLENCOURT at 4.0 P.M. Sgt. F.J. BERRISFORD dispatched to Base for discharge on termination of engagement. major F.G CROMPTON proceeded to ENGLAND on 24/4/16	
7/5/16	The Brigade (less 2nd Battery) left GRAND CAMP at 8.45 A.M. and marched to BERLENCOURT via BUNEVILLE, HOUVIN-HOUVIGNEUL arriving BERLENCOURT at 12.40 p.m. Lt. Col. GISBORNE proceeded to 3rd Army Infantry School AUXI LE CHATEAU to attend conference. Major BUXTON-SMITH assumed temporary command of the Brigade Lts.W.K.S. HASLAM Lys. BATES & LOWE & Dr. BASSETT proceeded on leave to ENGLAND 8/5/16 to 15/5/16	

Army Form C. 2118.

WAR DIARY
or
INTELLIGENCE SUMMARY.
(Erase heading not required.)

Instructions regarding War Diaries and Intelligence
Summaries are contained in F. S. Regs., Part II.
and the Staff Manual respectively. Title pages
will be prepared in manuscript.

Hour, Date, Place	Summary of Events and Information	Remarks and References to Appendices
In the Field 7/5/16 (cont)	The 2nd DERBY Battery left BERLENCOURT & marched to WARLINCOURT arriving there at 4.0 p.m.	MWh
8/5/16.	Showery with bright intervals. Showery day. The Brigade less 2nd DERBY Battery left BERLENCOURT at 7.30 AM and marched to WARLINCOURT via GRAND RULLECOURT, SOMBRIN, SAULTY, COUTURELLE, LA BELLEVUE arriving WARLINCOURT at 11.15 AM. hour F.M. Joyce returned from leave. One Section 2nd Batty marched into action of FONQUE VILLERS guns being in position at 9.30 P.M.	F.M.J
9.5.16	Rain. Brigade and Battery commanders reconnoitred positions	F.M.J
10.5.16	Fine day. Remaining Section of 2nd Batty marched into action at FONQUEVILLERS guns being in position at 9.30 P.M. Working parties proceeded to 1st and R Batty gun positions Capt H.L. NEWTON promoted Major (TEMPY). hint WKS HASLAM Promoted captain (TEMPY).	F.M.J
11.5.16	Fine day. B.Q.M.S. PARTNER, Bar WOODWARD, G.W. GODWIN and Dr BACON, HEGG, HILTON, SWEENEY, proceeded on sent-leave to ENGLAND via HAVRE 12.5.16 to 19.5.16	F.M.J

Army Form C. 2118.

WAR DIARY
or
INTELLIGENCE SUMMARY
(Erase heading not required.)

Instructions regarding War Diaries and Intelligence Summaries are contained in F. S. Regs., Part II. and the Staff Manual respectively. Title pages will be prepared in manuscript.

Hour, Date, Place	Summary of Events and Information	Remarks and References to Appendices
In the field		
12.5.16	Fine day. 2/Lieut BURRA returned from LARKHILL Course and leave	F.M.J
13.5.16	Showery. Lieut Col GISBORNE returned from commanding Officers conference at 3rd Army Infantry School. The nomenclature of the Brigade was changed to 233rd Brigade R.F.A. The Batteries being lettered "A", "B", and "R"	F.M.J
14.5.16	Dull fine day.	F M J
15.5.16	Wet day. Gnr MITCHELL and Drs JONES, COLLIS, CARTER, GORMAN and WIBBERLEY proceeded on Scat' leave to ENGLAND 16.5.16 to 23.5.16. Brigade Head Quarters moved forward to SOUASTRE. Lieut J.M. SPURRIER returned from leave "R" Battery fired on the following targets K3b 9½, Tow Z, E28c 6½, 3½, E23c 6.7, E29a 1.½, E28c 6½, 3½, K3d 7.7, GOMMECOURT WOOD E23c 6.7, and E28c 6½. 3/2	F. M. J

Army Form C. 2118.

WAR DIARY
or
INTELLIGENCE SUMMARY
(Erase heading not required.)

Instructions regarding War Diaries and Intelligence Summaries are contained in F. S. Regs, Part II. and the Staff Manual respectively. Title pages will be prepared in manuscript.

Hour, Date, Place	Summary of Events and Information	Remarks and References to Appendices
In the field 16.5.16	Fine day. "B" Batty fired on the following targets K3d 7.7, T8a Z, E28c 6½.3½ E29a 1.½ GOMMERCOURT VILLAGE	F.M.J
17.5.16	Fine day "B" Batty fired 44 rounds at various targets	F.M.J
18.5.16	Fine day "B" Batty registered the following targets E24a 1½.4½, E18c 7.1½, E18c 8.2. Sergt POTTER and Gnr LONGDON proceeded with guns to Artillery School HAUTECLOQUE to act as instructors.	F.M.J
19.5.16	Fine day. Ranyadi commander proceeded to reconnoitre gun positions for the corps line. 2/Lieut BLISS, TPR WILLIAMS, Gnr INGRAM and WRIGHT and Dr HANDLEY, CREED.C. and DEUCHAR (958) proceeded on scout leave to ENGLAND via HAVRE. 20.5.16 to 28.5.16. "B" Batty fired on following targets. Tracks at E29 central E28c 6½.3½. K4b 3.7. and K3b 9.½ , cross roads F19c.8.1	F.M.J
20.5.16	Fine day "B" Batty fired on following targets. Road junction E28d 10½.2. Communication trench at E29 q 0.2 to 3.7 cross roads at F.19 c.8.1. and trench mortar at K3b 9½.2.0	F.M.J

Army Form C. 2118.

WAR DIARY
or
INTELLIGENCE SUMMARY
(Erase heading not required.)

Instructions regarding War Diaries and Intelligence Summaries are contained in F. S. Regs., Part II. and the Staff Manual respectively. Title pages will be prepared in manuscript.

Hour, Date, Place	Summary of Events and Information	Remarks and References to Appendices
In the field 21.5.16	Fine day. Received orders concerning reorganisation of 46th DIVISIONAL ARTILLERY. "B" Battery fired on following targets to register and silence trench mortars F.26d 2.1, K.4 c 2.0.-8.5, to K.4 c 9.4, K.4 d 1.8.-9.4 to K.4 d 8.0.-4.5 K.6 b 9.9 and E.28.C 64.-3/2. Lieut E.S. HASLAM and Sergt WITT.H. proceeded to Artillery School HAUTECLOQUE for course.	F.M.J
22.5.16	Fine day	
23.5.16	Fine day. "A" Battery transferred to 230 Brigade R.F.A. ⎫ "B" Battery " " 232 Brigade R.F.A. ⎬ Authority "C" Battery " " 231 Brigade R.F.A. ⎭ G.H.Q No O.B. 818 Ammo col ⎫ two officers ⎬ A Echelon 46 D.A.C. d/ 6.5.16 + B.S.M Hardy C ⎭ D Battys of 230, 231 and 232 Brigades R.F.A transferred to form 233 Brigade R.F.A., under original 233 Brigade Head Quarters staff and known as "A", "B" and "C" Battys. Authority G.H.Q No OB 818 d/ 6.5.16 Capt G.D.WILSON and 2/Lieut F.T.JONES attached to the new A/233 Batty, and the new C/233 Batty respectively. B.S.M HARDY. C transferred to 231 Brigade R.F.A	F.M.J

Army Form C. 2118.

WAR DIARY
or
INTELLIGENCE SUMMARY.
(Erase heading not required.)

Instructions regarding War Diaries and Intelligence Summaries are contained in F. S. Regs., Part II. and the Staff Manual respectively. Title pages will be prepared in manuscript.

Hour, Date, Place	Summary of Events and Information	Remarks and References to Appendices
In the field 23.5.16 (cont)	2/Lieut C.H. ARKWRIGHT, Gnr SCHIROKEY and Dr CLARKE, HOCKHAM, WOOD, and GIBSON. proceeded on Short leave to ENGLAND 24.5.16 to 31.5.16. 25 reinforcements joined the Brigade	F.M.J.
24.5.16	Fine day. Batteries sent working parties to their new positions. C.R.A inspected Guns transferred to "C" Batty from 232 Bde Ammn col	F.M.J
25.5.16	Showery.	F.M.J
26.5.16	Showery.	F.M.J
27.5.16	Fine day. Lieut A.F. DUFTON, Cpl LEE, Gnrs BRIGGS, ECCLESTONE and HANCOCK and Dr GRAVES and ROBINSON proceeded on Short leave to ENGLAND via HAVRE 28.5.16 to 5.6.16. 1 Filter and 3 Saddles joined from 46" D.A.C	F.M.J

Army Form C. 2118.

WAR DIARY
or
INTELLIGENCE SUMMARY
(Erase heading not required.)

Instructions regarding War Diaries and Intelligence Summaries are contained in F. S. Regs., Part II. and the Staff Manual respectively. Title pages will be prepared in manuscript.

Hour, Date, Place	Summary of Events and Information	Remarks and references to Appendices
In the field		
28.5.16	Fine day.	F.M.J
29.5.16	Fine day	F.M.J
30.5.16	Wet early, fine later	F.M.J
31.5.16	Fine day	
	2/Lieut F.T.Jones, Bdr OTTEWELL Gnrs BOWERMAN, GURBUTT Drs WHITE and DONE proceeded on leave to ENGLAND 1.6.16 to 8.6.16	F.M.J

Lionel Antrim
LIEUT.COL. R.F.A.
COMDG. 233RD BRIGADE, R.F.A.

CONFIDENTIAL.

WAR DIARY.

HEAD QUARTERS

233rd: BRIGADE. R.F.A.

JUNE 1st: to JUNE 30th: 1916.

CONFIDENTIAL.

WAR DIARY
of
233RD BRIGADE, R.F.A.

June 1916.

F. M. Joyce Lieut for Lieut-Col. R.F.A.
Comdg. 233rd Brigade, R.F.A.

Army Form C. 2118.

WAR DIARY
or
INTELLIGENCE SUMMARY.
(Erase heading not required.)

Instructions regarding War Diaries and Intelligence Summaries are contained in F. S. Regs., Part II. and the Staff Manual respectively. Title pages will be prepared in manuscript.

Hour, Date, Place	Summary of Events and Information	Remarks and References to Appendices
In the field 1.6.16	Fine day. 2/Lieut COOKE proceeded to ENGLAND 2.6.16 to 9.6.16	F.M.J.
2.6.16	Fine day	F.M.J.
3.6.16	Fine day Lieut Col L.G GISBORNE awarded the C.M.G.	F.M.J.
4.6.16	Fine day Captain G.D. WILSON a/Bdr DAVIES S. Gnrs HILL W.H. WENTWORTH HIGGINS, DEELEY, HALL, STANWAY, HOLLOWAY, LAUGHTON, EARDLEY and MARSH and Dr HEATH LUDLAM, CASHMERE, SAMWAYS, NAYLOR and PHILLIPS proceeded on Scot leave to ENGLAND 6.6.16 to 13.6.16	F.M.J
5.6.16	Fine day Lieut Col GISBORNE proceeded on Scot leave to ENGLAND 6.6.13 to 13.6.16.	F.M.J

Army Form C. 2118.

WAR DIARY
or
INTELLIGENCE SUMMARY
(Erase heading not required.)

Instructions regarding War Diaries and Intelligence Summaries are contained in F. S. Regs., Part II. and the Staff Manual respectively. Title pages will be prepared in manuscript.

Hour, Date, Place	Summary of Events and Information	Remarks and references to Appendices
In the field 6.6.16	Fine day	F.M.J
7.6.16	Showery. 15 Other Ranks Surplus returned to Base and 11 other ranks transferred to 46th D.A.C	FMJ
8.6.16	Showery	FMJ
9.6.16	Showery. Personnel earmarked for Heavy Trench Mortar Battery proceeded to 232nd Bde R.F.A. Gnrs ROBERTS, PATCHETT, GRICE, GRASHLEY, READ, LONGBOTTOM and Drs BISHOP, BIRKS, FLETCHER proceeded on Staff leave to ENGLAND 10.6.16 to 17.6.16	FMJ
10.6.16	Showery. Lieut C MORRIS rejoined from Gotfinel.	FMJ
11.6.16	Showery	FMJ

(9 29 6) W 3332—1107 100,000 10/13 H W V Forms/C. 2118/10.

Army Form C. 2118.

WAR DIARY
or
INTELLIGENCE SUMMARY.
(Erase heading not required.)

Instructions regarding War Diaries and Intelligence Summaries are contained in F. S. Regs., Part II. and the Staff Manual respectively. Title pages will be prepared in manuscript.

Hour, Date, Place	Summary of Events and Information	Remarks and references to Appendices
In the field 12.6.16	Scenery	F.M.T
13.6.16	Scenery. Gnrs. WHITACRE, COOK, WELLS, SMITH WARDLE, CATTLING and Drs. HODSON, ROSE, PEACH, FOLEY, TALBOT (promoted on 5cant leave to ENGLAND 14.6.16 to 21.6.16. Lieut Col L.G GISBORNE returned from leave. "A" Batty went into action at K2 C 4.8. (Syd NE¹/20,000) the guns being in position 11 P.M.	F.M.T.
14.6.16	Scenery. "B" Batty (3 guns) went into action at J 6 L 84.49 (Syd NE¹/20,000) guns being in position at 9.15 P.M. At 11 P.M. all watches were adjusted one hour, making 11 P.M. ~~noon~~ midnight. Lieut A. LIGHTFOOT and 2/Lieut F.J. STEWARD joined the Brigade and posted to "C" and "A" Batty's respectively.	F.M.T
15.6.16	D/ue "C" Batty went into action at E20.C.0.2.5 (Syd NE¹/20,000) guns being in position at 11 P.M. A Batty fired 84 rounds to register registered line for all guns.	F.M.T.

Army Form C. 2118.

WAR DIARY
or
~~INTELLIGENCE SUMMARY.~~
(Erase heading not required.)

Instructions regarding War Diaries and Intelligence Summaries are contained in F. S. Regs., Part II. and the Staff Manual respectively. Title pages will be prepared in manuscript.

Hour, Date, Place	Summary of Events and Information	Remarks and References to Appendices
	No rain fired	
16.6.16	Fine day. 'B' Battery fired on E28d 3.5. to register	F.M.T
17.6.16	Fine day 'A' Battery fired 40 rounds to register wire and on second line Trenches 'B' Battery fired on E25b 3.3. to b.54. and point E28 b 18.08. 'C' Battery fired on E28C 6.4 and E28C 8.9. to register	F.M.T
18.6.16	Fine day 'A' Battery fired on wire in front of E28 a 1/2.9 and on 2nd line trench E28 d.7 to E28 c.7.2 and on trench E28c 4.5 to E28d 5.0. 'B' Battery fired on front line from E28 d.09 to E28 b 60.45. and 2nd line from E28 d 34.94 to E28 b 85.28. registration good too his premature. 'C' Battery registered E28C 6.4. E28C 6.4. one premature. 4th gun of B Battery proceeded into action Brigade H.Q. moved into dugouts at LA HAIE CHATEAU.	F.M.T

WAR DIARY
~~INTELLIGENCE SUMMARY~~

(Erase heading not required.)

Army Form C. 2118.

Instructions regarding War Diaries and Intelligence Summaries are contained in F. S. Regs., Part II. and the Staff Manual respectively. Title pages will be prepared in manuscript.

Hour, Date, Place	Summary of Events and Information	Remarks and references to Appendices
In the field 19.6.16	Fine day "A" Batty registered wire infront of enemy fire trench E.28.c.6.10; communication trenches E.28.c.5.5 to E.28.d.50.05 and Second line trench E.28.d.27.6. E.28.b.7.2. Also obtained Cuts on Suspected OPs "B" Batty registered 4" gun on various targets "C" Batty fired on E.28.c.6.4. and E.28.c.5.4.	F.M.T.
20.6.16	Fine day. "C" Batty fired on E.28.c.6.4. and on enemy's wire E.28.c.5.4.	F.M.T.
21.6.16	Fine day "B" Batty registered point E.28.b.45.35 "C" Batty fired on datum point E.28.c.6.4. and E.28.c.5.4	F.M.T.

WAR DIARY
or
INTELLIGENCE SUMMARY

(Erase heading not required.)

Army Form C. 2118.

Instructions regarding War Diaries and Intelligence Summaries are contained in F. S. Regs., Part II. and the Staff Manual respectively. Title pages will be prepared in manuscript.

Hour, Date, Place	Summary of Events and Information	Remarks and References to Appendices
In the field 22.6.16.	Fine day. "A" Battery fired on try enemy 4.2 battery no material damage done. "B" Battery registered east edge of GOMMECOURT WOOD "C" Battery fired on station (point E28c5.44. and aeroplane target N°9 (K4 b 15.90)	F.M.T.
23.6.16	Showery "B" Battery checked all registrations in E28b and E28d front line communication trenches and S.P. Supports "C" Battery fired on E28c5.4.	F.M.T.
24.6.16	Showery. A Battery fired 535 rounds Shrapnel and 10 rounds H.E. on wire cutting and various bombardments (U day) "B" Battery fired 80 shrapnel and 52 H.E. on various bombardments (U day) "C" Battery fired 24 H Shrapnel and 79 H.E. wire cutting and various bombardments (U day). Results of all batteries satisfactory	F.M.T.

Army Form C. 2118.

WAR DIARY
or
INTELLIGENCE SUMMARY.
(Erase heading not required.)

Instructions regarding War Diaries and Intelligence Summaries are contained in F. S. Regs, Part II. and the Staff Manual respectively. Title pages will be prepared in manuscript.

Hour, Date, Place	Summary of Events and Information	Remarks and References to Appendices
In the field		
25.6.16	Fine day.	
	"B" Batty 323 rounds shrapnel and 306 HE wire cutting and various bombardments (V day)	F.M.J.
	"C" Batty 181 Shrapnel and 441 HE on various bombardments (V day)	
	Fire of both batteries reported satisfactory	
26.6.16	Showery.	
	"A" Batty fired 380 Shrapnel and 1155 HE on wire cutting and various bombardments (W day)	F.M.J.
	"B" Batty fired 278 shrapnel and 665 HE on various bombardments (W day)	
	"C" Batty fired 552 shrapnel and 520 HE on wire cutting and various bombardments	

(9 29 6) W 3332—1107 100,000 10/13 H W V Forms/C. 2118/10.

WAR DIARY
or
INTELLIGENCE SUMMARY
(Erase heading not required.)

Army Form C. 2118.

Hour, Date, Place	Summary of Events and Information	Remarks and References to Appendices
In the field	5 enemy	
27.6.16	Major F.R COLLIS "B" Battery wounded	
	"A" Battery fired 1150 Shrapnel and 894 H.E. on wire etc (X day) cutting good "lane" 80 feet wide	F. M Joyce
	"B" Battery fired 660 Shrapnel and 904 H.E on various bombardments (X day)	
	"C" Battery fired 760 Shrapnel and 686 H.E on various bombardments and wire cutting (X day)	
	Lieut Col L.G. GISBORNE proceeded to advanced infantry Head Quarters as LIAISON Officer.	
28.6.16	0 enemy	
	"A" Battery fired 905 Shrapnel and 160 HE on Trenches and wire cutting	
	"B" Battery fired 754 Shrapnel and 868 HE on various bombardments and wire cutting (Y day)	F.M.J.
	"C" Battery fired 1227 Shrapnel and 773 HE on wire cutting and various bombardments (Y day)	
	Lieut Col L.G. GISBORNE returned from advanced H.Q. operations being postponed	

Army Form C. 2118.

WAR DIARY
or
INTELLIGENCE SUMMARY
(Erase heading not required.)

Hour, Date, Place	Summary of Events and Information	Remarks and References to Appendices
In the field	Fine day	
29.6.16	One man wounded, One Curto Gired and two Curto wounded (Dr. Cox)	
	"A" Batty delivering ammunition.	F.M.T
	2/Lt LEES and Gnrs BRYAN, SMITH, and ABEY "B" Batty wounded	
	"A" Batty fired 683 Shrapnel and 531 HE Wire cutting (Y1 day)	
	"B" Batty fired 283 Shrapnel and 1478 HE on Various bombardments (Y1 day)	
	"C" Batty fired 576 Shrapnel and 368 HE on Wire cutting and Various bombardments (Y1 day)	
	Lieut Col. L.G. GISBORNE proceeded to advanced infantry Head Quarters	
30.6.16	Fine day	
	2/Lieut COOKE proceeded to ENGLAND ceasing to be attached to the Brigade (currently G.H.Q)	F.M.T
	"A" Batty fired 1097 Shrapnel and 446 HE bombardments and Wire cutting	
	"B" Batty fired 67 Shrapnel and 100 HE on bombardments and registration	
	"B" Batty had three guns temporarily out of action	
	"C" Batty fired 78 Shrapnel and 541 HE on Various bombardments (½ day)	

Leop Patana Lt.Col. R.F.A.
Comdg. 233rd. Brigade, R.F.A.

CONFIDENTIAL.

WAR DIARY.

233rd: BRIGADE. R.F.A.

July 1st: to July 31st: 1916.

Army Form C. 2118.

WAR DIARY
or
~~INTELLIGENCE SUMMARY~~
(Erase heading not required.)

Instructions regarding War Diaries and Intelligence Summaries are contained in F. S. Regs., Part II. and the Staff Manual respectively. Title pages will be prepared in manuscript.

Hour, Date, Place	Summary of Events and Information	Remarks and References to Appendices
In the field 1.7.16	Fine day. All three Batteries fired a large number of rounds on the various tasks allotted to them for Z day. Gnr PRIME "B" Batty killed. Gnr WHITELAM "A" Batty wound chest	F.M.J.
2.7.16	Fine day. B Battery fired on E23 d B.6. to Kregeli guns which had temporarily been out of action. Lieut Col L.G. GISBORNE C.M.G. and telegraphists returned from advanced infantry Head Quarters	F.M.J
3.7.16	Fine day. Quiet on our front. "B" Batty stirred on occasions during the day. Brigade and Battery commanders proceeded to reconnoitre knees and positions of 126 Brigade R.F.A. at POMMIERS. The General of one Section of "A" "B" and "C" Batteries proceed to relieve the personal of one Section A.B. and C Batteries 126th Bde One Section of guns withdrawn from Fort Butte and proceeded to wagon lines. The Section of A Batty was relieved by a Section of C/282 Bde R.F.A. guns being covered over	F.M.J.

Army Form C. 2118.

WAR DIARY
or
INTELLIGENCE SUMMARY

(Erase heading not required.)

Hour, Date, Place	Summary of Events and Information	Remarks and references to Appendices
In the field 4.7.16	W.J. day. Major F.R Collis returned from Corbie Remaining Sections of "A" "B" and "C" Batts. proceeded to relieve remaining sections of "A" "B" & "C" Batts. 126 Bde. Remaining Section C/282 marched into "C" Batty position guns being handed over. The guns of remaining Sections of B and C Battys withdrawn and proceeded to Souzger Wood. Brigade Head Quarters proceeded to SOUASTRE command being handed over to Northern Group 56th Division artillery at 6 P.M. All Batteries checked registration	F.M.J
5.7.16	Fine day Brigade Head Quarters proceeded to POMMIER command being taken over from 126 Bde. R.F.A at 6 A.M. The guns of "B" and "C" Battys were handed over to 37th Division artillery. The guns of A, B, and C Battys 126 Bde R.F.A. taken over by A B and C Battys 233rd Bde A Battery fired 10 rounds on road East of MONCHY B Battery fired 19 rounds for registration purposes "C" Batty fired 15 rounds on W29 b 45.75 and W29 b 46.50	F.M.J

Army Form C. 2118.

WAR DIARY
or
INTELLIGENCE SUMMARY
(Erase heading not required.)

Instructions regarding War Diaries and Intelligence Summaries are contained in F. S. Regs., Part II. and the Staff Manual respectively. Title pages will be prepared in manuscript.

Hour, Date, Place	Summary of Events and Information	Remarks and References to Appendices
In the field 6.7.16	Fine day. "B" Battery fired 59 Shrapnel and 2 HE on enemy front line Trenches. "C" Battery fired on following targets X7d 10.60, W12d 80.20, X7c 10.80, and X7d 20.60, for registration and repriment	F M Joye
7.7.16	Fine day. "A" Battery fired on enemy front line and communication trenches and verified reference lines "B" Battery fires on enemy front line at various times during the day. "C" Battery fired on E2q 6 45.95 to registrate	FMJ
8.7.16	Wet day. "A" Battery fires on enemy front line and communication trenches "B" Battery fired on enemy front line for repriment "C" Battery fired to registrate on following targets on register and left of zone W29b 40.85, W29b 40.50, W30a 90.25, W23d 85.60, W29b 08.32, W29b 1.1.	FMJ

Army Form C. 2118.

WAR DIARY
or
INTELLIGENCE SUMMARY
(Erase heading not required.)

Instructions regarding War Diaries and Intelligence Summaries are contained in F. S. Regs., Part II. and the Staff Manual respectively. Title pages will be prepared in manuscript.

Hour, Date, Place	Summary of Events and Information	Remarks and References to Appendices
In the field 8.7.16 continued	Brigade Wagon Lines moved from GAUDIEMPRE to LA HERLIERE.	F. M J
9.7.16	Fine day. "A" Battery fired at enemy M.C. at E5d 45.20 at Support O.P. at E5a 4.5. and Suspected M.G. E5a 2.2½. "B" Battery fired in retaliation on enemy front line "C" Battery fired X 13a 40.90, X 13a 35.20, X 7d 20.60 and W 18 b 8.5 W. ammunition used. Lieut ADSHEAD proceeded on course at 3rd Army Artillery School HAUTECLOQUE. Lieut A. LIGHTFOOT proceeded on course at 3rd Army School of mortars. Sadd O'MEARA proceeded to Base being medically age	F. MJ
10.7.16	Fine day One Section "A" Battery relieved by one Section C/84 Bde RFA at 5.3 P.M. and the relieved Section proceeded to relieve one Section A/231 Bde RFA One Section "B" Battery relieved by one Section A/124 Bde RFA at 5.50 P.M. and the relieved Section proceeded to relieve one Section C/231 Bde RFA	F.M.J.

WAR DIARY
or
INTELLIGENCE SUMMARY
(Erase heading not required.)

Army Form C. 2118.

Instructions regarding War Diaries and Intelligence Summaries are contained in F. S. Regs., Part II. and the Staff Manual respectively. Title pages will be prepared in manuscript.

Hour, Date, Place	Summary of Events and Information	Remarks and References to Appendices
In the field 10.7.16 continued	"B" Batty fired 6 rounds in retaliation on E5a 67 and registered Suspected M.C. emplacement. "C" Batty fired on W29b 40.85, W29b 40.50, and W29b 08.32.	F.M.J.
11.7.16	Fine day "C" Batty fired on X7c 65.75. X7c 10.99. W29b 45.75. W29b 2.3. and W29b 3.4. Remaining Sections of "A" and "B" Battys relieved by remaining Sections of C/124 Bde RFA and A/124 Bde RFA respectively, guns being handed over. The relieved Sections of "A" and "B" Battys proceed to relieve the remaining Sections of "A" and "C" Battys 231 Bde R.F.A., guns being taken over. Brigade Head Quarters proceed to BERLES-AU-BOIS.	F.M.J

Army Form C. 2118.

WAR DIARY
or
INTELLIGENCE SUMMARY
(Erase heading not required.)

Instructions regarding War Diaries and Intelligence Summaries are contained in F. S. Regs., Part II. and the Staff Manual respectively. Title pages will be prepared in manuscript.

Hour, Date, Place	Summary of Events and Information	Remarks and References to Appendices
In the field		
12.7.16	Fine day	
	A Battery fired on enemy front line and Support Trenches and checked registration	
	"B" Batty carried out registration. Quantity of ammunition not satisfactory	F.M.J.
	"C" Batty fired on W2g6 45.75, X19c 14.83, X7c 2.9, and X7d 10.60 in retaliation and cut a 20 yards lane of wire at W2 3 d 8 9 .8 4 and kept lane open during the night	
13.7.16	Fine day	
	All Batteries registered for and carried out special bombardment in support of discharge of gas	F.M.J.
14.7.16	Fine day.	
	All Batteries registered for and carried out special bombardment for raid on enemy Trenches	F.M.J.
	F.G.S.S. MASON E "B" Batty proceeded to Base (Auth DAG Base No 2996)	

Army Form C. 2118.

WAR DIARY
or
INTELLIGENCE SUMMARY
(Erase heading not required.)

Hour, Date, Place	Summary of Events and Information	Remarks and References to Appendices
In the field 15.7.16	Fine day. Lieut. Col. L.G. GISBORNE took over command of RIGHT GROUP at 3 A.M. composed of A and B/233 R.S.C/233 A and C/232 Rs D/232 and RSD/230 "A" Battery moved position to E2.d 25.70 and registered their zone "B" Battery fired on points in front line trenches at E11b and E5c and E5d. One gun of A Battery damaged by shell fire. All Batteries fired in Special bombardment at night. Head Quarters moved to POMMIER	F.M.J
16.7.16.	Fine day B Battery fired 19 rounds M.G. emplacement E5d 05.36 and ryger of zone E11b 55.35. "C" Battery fired 8 rounds on F.16 H.6. in cooperation with D/230 hit A LIGHT FOOT returned from trench mortar emire	F.M.J
17.7.16	Fine day. "B" Battery fired on enemy front line + Supports in E5d and O.Ps F.id 55.48 and F.id 70.50. "C" Battery fired on X7d 15.70 X7c 35.95. X7c 00.25. All Batterys fired in Special bombardment	F.M.J

Army Form C. 2118

WAR DIARY
or
INTELLIGENCE SUMMARY
(Erase heading not required.)

Instructions regarding War Diaries and Intelligence Summaries are contained in F.S. Regs., Part II. and the Staff Manual respectively. Title Pages will be prepared in manuscript.

Place	Date	Hour	Summary of Events and Information	Remarks and references to Appendices
In the field	18.7.16		Wet day. 1 Sergt. and 4 cpls (Sergt. F.C. TAYLOR 1106 Cpls E. BURNELL 894 T.H. WIDLAKE 1016 P. ALDRIDGE 2411 and FLOYD 2224 joined Brigade as reinforcements from 48th Base Depot and posted as follows Sergt TAYLOR and Cpl BURNELL to "C" Batty remainder to "B" Batty "B" Batty fired on enemy front line E5a 50.00 to E5a 20.10 C Batty fired on X18c 80.50. and X13a 60.60. to Caravan and apparent the enemy all batteries fired on gun communication concentration scheme Zone (E5a 50.00 to E5a 20.10) and at night in bombardment of enemy's trenches and dumps.	F.M.T
	19.7.16		Fine day. "A" Batty fired on enemy front line and failed enemy ammunition "B" Batty fired on enemy front line W29b 20.25 to W29b 30.40. and on M.G. emplacement at E5c 9.5. "C" Batty fired on following targets W29b 35.40 W29b 43.55 W29b 40.50. W29b 45.75 W29b 45.45.	F.M.T
	20.7.16		Fine day A Batty B Batty } registered for and carried out three special bombardments C Batty } at 6:30 P.M. 7:0 P.M. and 9:25 P.M.	F.M.T

WAR DIARY or INTELLIGENCE SUMMARY

Army Form C. 2118

(Erase heading not required.)

Place	Date	Hour	Summary of Events and Information	Remarks and references to Appendices
In the field	21.7.16		Fine day. "A" Battery registered lewis gun nests on enemy front line.	
			"A" Battery fired on enemy front line and supports in retaliation.	F.M.J
			C Battery fired as well as other Batterys in organised retaliation on MONCHY	
	22.7.16		Fine day. "A" Battery retaliated on enemy front line.	
			"B" Battery fired on X.7.c 20.90 W.29.b 40.85 W.23.d 9.5 W.18.b 6.5.18. and W.12.d 80.20	F.M.J
	23.7.16		Fine day. "A" Battery fired a few rounds on enemy working party and registered Target 1.25.27 and 73 by Aeroplane.	
			B Battery registered Barrage 5c.	F.M.J

Army Form C. 2118

WAR DIARY
or
~~INTELLIGENCE SUMMARY~~

(Erase heading not required.)

Place	Date	Hour	Summary of Events and Information	Remarks and references to Appendices
In the field	24.7.16		Fine day. Wagon lines of A & B Batteries moved to LA BAZEQUE FARM. The Corps Commander visited "C" Battery wagon lines. A Battery fired 12 rounds at enemy working party and 30 rounds on enemy front line opposite trench 99 to recognize French gun.	F.M.J.
	25.7.16		Fine day. "A" Battery fired a few rounds on enemy front line. "B" Battery fired on Eastern entrances of MONCHY and rated from E 6 a 2.3 to E 6 d 0.5. and also fired for retaliation for T.M. fire. "C" Battery fired on X 7 c 40.95 and W 12 d 8.2. H.Q. Wagon lines moved to LA BAZEQUE FARM. The Corps Commander visited "A" and "B" Battery wagon lines.	F.M.J.
	26.7.16		Fine day. "A" Battery fired on enemy front line for aggravation, in retaliation and as a test at request of infantry. "B" Batty fired on E 5 C 15.35 and E 5 d 7.8.	F.M.J

Army Form C. 2118

WAR DIARY
or
INTELLIGENCE SUMMARY
(Erase heading not required.)

Instructions regarding War Diaries and Intelligence Summaries are contained in F.S. Regs., Part II. and the Staff Manual respectively. Title Pages will be prepared in manuscript.

Place	Date	Hour	Summary of Events and Information	Remarks and references to Appendices
In the field	27.7.16		Fine day	
			"A" Battery fired on enemy front line	
			"C" Battery fired on X1d 90.45, X2d 20.98, W29b 40.85, W29b 40.50 and W29b 08.32.	F.M.J
	28.7.16		Fine day	
			"A" Battery demonstration for the training of Infantry Officers	
			"B" Battery fired 15 rounds on E11b 80.90 for Aeroplane registration	
			"C" Battery carried out K.K. call at 7.32 P.M.	F.M.J
	29.7.16		Fine day	
			"A" Battery reregistered No 2 Gun and carried out K.K. call at 8.45 P.M.	
			"C" Battery registered by aeroplane W29 b 45.50 b W29 b 70.30 and F1 d 90.15	
			"B" Battery carried out special bombardment against enemy transport	F.M.J
	30.7.16		Fine day	
			"C" Battery fired on W29 b 13 and W29 b 45.75	F.M.J

Army Form C. 2118.

WAR DIARY
or
INTELLIGENCE SUMMARY.
(Erase heading not required.)

Instructions regarding War Diaries and Intelligence
Summaries are contained in F. S. Regs., Part II.
and the Staff Manual respectively. Title pages
will be prepared in manuscript.

Hour, Date, Place	Summary of Events and Information	Remarks and references to Appendices
In the field 31.7.16	Fine day 'A' Batty fired on enemy front line and Suffolk 'B' Batty fired on E 5 d 7.8. 'C' Batty fired on various targets at rear of infantry and in counter reprisal. Test concentrate M carried out at 11.3 AM Lieut. P.B. DUMBELL and W.A. PRICHARD, Sergt MEEDS and Cpl WIDLAKE proceeded to 116th Divisional artillery School for course [signature] Lieut-Col. R.F.A. Comdg. 233rd Brigade, R.F.A.	F M J

CONFIDENTIAL.

WAR DIARY.

233rd: Brigade. R.F.A.

AUGUST 1st: to AUGUST 31st: 1916.

Army Form C. 2118.

WAR DIARY
or
~~INTELLIGENCE SUMMARY.~~
(Erase heading not required.)

Instructions regarding War Diaries and Intelligence
Summaries are contained in F. S. Regs., Part II.
and the Staff Manual respectively. Title pages
will be prepared in manuscript.

Hour, Date, Place	Summary of Events and Information	Remarks and references to Appendices
In the field 1.8.16	Fine day. "A" Battery supplied covering fire for our Trench Mortars "B" Battery fired on E5 d 3.2. E5 d 8.8. F.16.2.2. and E5 c 15.25 "C" Battery fired on W2 q b 2.3. and on F.1.d 90.15 by aeroplane. All Batts carried out Priority test Co-ordinates M at 3.58 P.M. No 1691 Dr SHELLEY "C" Battery proceeded to ABBEVILLE for farriery course at No 22 Veterinary Hospital. Lieut A LIGHTFOOT and Servant posted to "Z" 46 T.M. Battery.	FMJ
2.8.16	Fine day. No 14.05 Gnr PERRY E "C" Battery attached 16" Anti Aircraft Battery for course. Information received that No 38 Sergt BETTANY H "B" Battery and No 1537 Gnr KENYON R "A" Batty have been awarded MILITARY MEDAL (Gazette 3rd Army H.R./157) "A" Battery fired on enemy front line "B" Battery fired on following targets registering by aeroplane F.7a 4.5.t.o, E12 b.50.10 E5 d 8.9. F.1.d 90.15 "C" Batty fired on enemy's works at W.12 d 10.25, X7 c 2.6. and X7 c 30.10	FMJ

(9 29 6) W 3332—1107 100,000 10/13 H W V Forms/C. 2118/10.

Army Form C. 2118.

WAR DIARY
or
INTELLIGENCE SUMMARY
(Erase heading not required.)

Instructions regarding War Diaries and Intelligence Summaries are contained in F. S. Regs., Part II. and the Staff Manual respectively. Title pages will be prepared in manuscript.

Hour, Date, Place	Summary of Events and Information	Remarks and references to Appendices
In the field 3.8.16	Fine day "A" Batty registered gun which had been temporarily out of action "B" Batty, I.O.M carried out tests with weak springs and special buffer oil "C" Batty fired on W24 c 7520 and W23 d 9194. Private CLULOW R.A.M.C N515 D{}^{r} SMITH.G. and B° 1285 D{}^{r} DEELEY.J. proceeded to Sanitary School for course	F.M.J
4. 8.16	Fine day All Batts fired in response to S.O.S call given at 3.45 A.M by Right Battalion 138 infantry Bde. N° 1789 Bdr ORTON, N° 1144 D{}^{r} HADLEY.H. N° 75 Gur BATES and N° 2147 Gur 155 ITT proceeded on Signalling course at 138 infantry Bde. hinl P.W. ADSHEAD and several returned from 3rd Army Artillery School	F.M.T

Army Form C. 2118.

WAR DIARY
of
INTELLIGENCE SUMMARY.
(Erase heading not required.)

Instructions regarding War Diaries and Intelligence Summaries are contained in F. S. Regs., Part II. and the Staff Manual respectively. Title pages will be prepared in manuscript.

Hour, Date, Place	Summary of Events and Information	Remarks and references to Appendices
In the field 5.8.16	Fine day, but cooler. Students from Divisional School visited "C" Batty. All batteries registered for Special operation. Between 11.5 PM and 11.50 PM all batteries performed Special bombardment laid down for raid by infantry on enemy front line trenches. Infantry reported that the barrage was very accurate and effective.	F.M.J
6.8.16	Fine day. Major COLLIS and Capt G.D. WILSON and Servants and Sgt HADLEY proceeded on a cruise to 3rd Army Artillery School. "C" Batty fired on W29b 2.2 in Support of our aeroplane flying low.	F.M.J
7.8.16	Fine day. "A" Batty and "C" Batty supplied covering fire for trench Mortars while firing.	F.M.J

Army Form C. 2118.

WAR DIARY
or
INTELLIGENCE SUMMARY.
(Erase heading not required.)

Instructions regarding War Diaries and Intelligence Summaries are contained in F. S. Regs., Part II. and the Staff Manual respectively. Title pages will be prepared in manuscript.

Hour, Date, Place	Summary of Events and Information	Remarks and references to Appendices
In the field 8.8.16	Fine day. "A" and "C" Batty's fired in special bombardment of trenches & spots in enemy front line. PRIVATE CLULOW. R.A.M.C. No 513 Dr SMTH.G. and No 1285 Dr DEELEY.T. returned from Sanitary School.	F.M.T
9.8.16	Fine day. "A" Batty fired on W29b 45.75 F16 5.6. W29b 10.35 "C" Batty fired on W29b 45.75, W29b 15.38, W29b 45.55	F.M.T
10.8.16	Fine day. "A" Batty registered on our own front line and "no mans land" C Batty fired on X7c 3.9. W12 d.2.2. X7c 18. X7a 35.00	F.M.T
11.8.16	Fine day. "C" Batty fired on W12 d.2.2. W29 b 4.4 and W29 b 2.3	F.M.T

Army Form C. 2118.

WAR DIARY
or
INTELLIGENCE SUMMARY.
(Erase heading not required.)

Instructions regarding War Diaries and Intelligence Summaries are contained in F. S. Regs., Part II. and the Staff Manual respectively. Title pages will be prepared in manuscript.

Hour, Date, Place	Summary of Events and Information	Remarks and references to Appendices
In the field 12.8.16	Fine day. Very little shooting, except at working parties. The Brigade held Sports. "C" Battery won the Brigade tug-of-war competition, runs second in the open turn out.	P.A.
13.8.16	Fine day. Lieut. F.M. Joyce was attached to the VII Corps Staff for instruction. Lieut. P. ADSHEAD took over the duties of Adjutant. "C" Battery fired on a working party.	P.A.
14.8.16	Fine day. All batteries fired. A Battery 20rds B.6rds L.45rds. One of "B" battery's guns underwent a test by the I.O.M. "C" had two gunners and three Telephonists wounded 2310 Bdr. Mason, 2380 Gr. Sawyer, 2204 Gr. Jones, 2193 Dr. Jackson, 2165 Dr. Harrison, their servants returned from Div. ARTY School. also Sgt MEEDS, Sgt Harrison & Bachman. Lt. P.P. DUMBELL, Lt. PRITCHARD	P.A.

Army Form C. 2118.

WAR DIARY
INTELLIGENCE SUMMARY
(Erase heading not required.)

Instructions regarding War Diaries and Intelligence
Summaries are contained in F. S. Regs., Part II.
and the Staff Manual respectively. Title pages
will be prepared in manuscript.

Hour, Date, Place	Summary of Events and Information	Remarks and references to Appendices
In the field 15. 8. 16	Fine day but showery. LT FOSTER & serrant, 2nd LT E H PADMORE & servant SGTS 1106 F C TAYLOR and 900 SGT PLANT & batman proceeded to Divisional Artillery school. 2nd LT. COLLINS posted to "C" Battery. 9 Reinforcements posted to Brigade from Base (5 G A & 4 G B).	P.A.
16. 8. 16	WET day. 2nd W. TURNER posted to "A" BATTY	P.A.
17. 8. 16	Fine day but showery. "A" Battery fired on 60 rounds on tracks at night. "B" — gun was again tested by the I.O.M. W. PARKER was admitted to hospital	P.A.
18. 8. 16	Fine day. "C" Battery fired lines on working parties. "A" — in retaliation for enemy shelling	P.A.

Army Form C. 2118.

WAR DIARY
INTELLIGENCE SUMMARY.
(Erase heading not required.)

Instructions regarding War Diaries and Intelligence Summaries are contained in F. S. Regs., Part II. and the Staff Manual respectively. Title pages will be prepared in manuscript.

Hour, Date, Place	Summary of Events and Information	Remarks and references to Appendices
In the field 19.8.16	Fine but showery day. A.B&C batteries all fired in retaliation on MONCHY as per Corps order. 2/Lt O. PRITCHARD returned from hospital.	P.A.
20.8.16	Fine but with occasional showers. Church parade. CRA was present. "A" battery wagon. "A" battery fired 220 rounds on covering fire for a trench mortar bombardment. Driving competition	P.A.
21.8.16	Fine day, exceptionally quiet day, no hostile fire at all. "A" Battery was second in the Divisional driving competition. 2/Lt V.O. Cuff-Bown was the officer. A,B,&C batteries all fired rifle fire on an aeroplane.	P.A.

WAR DIARY
or
INTELLIGENCE SUMMARY.

(Erase heading not required.)

Army Form C. 2118.

Hour, Date, Place	Summary of Events and Information	Remarks and references to Appendices
In the field 22.8.16	Fine day. A.B.C. Batteries fired in retaliation. Grand order. 1 reinforcements posted to Brigade. 6 signallers & gunner Capt. MORRIS went on instr. to (6 Divisional Arty School)	PR.
23.8.16	Fine day. A.B.C. Batteries fired in reponse to an aeroplane test call. Lt PADMORE went to hospital. Gnr BOWES of a DAC party attached was wounded in the neck.	
24.8.16	Fine day. BOMMIER was shelled with about 40 4.2 shrap. Two horses & a cow were killed. C233 fired on a working party at X6 a 3.6	

Army Form C. 2118.

WAR DIARY
or
INTELLIGENCE SUMMARY.
(Erase heading not required.)

Instructions regarding War Diaries and Intelligence Summaries are contained in F. S. Regs., Part II. and the Staff Manual respectively. Title pages will be prepared in manuscript.

Hour, Date, Place	Summary of Events and Information	Remarks and references to Appendices
In the field 25.8.16	Fine day. Quiet day. A+B batteries fired 4+2 & 10 rds respectly. One remount arrived for Brigade	RA
26.8.16	Fine day with showers. Very quiet	RA
27.8.16	Wet day. Very quiet.	RA
28.8.16	Reorganisation scheme commenced. A/233 nightly relieved by A/232 battery & B/233 " " " A/231 -"- C/233 I detachmr " A/232 " The two sections the detachments proceeded to their new positions were taken over by their new batteries respectively.	RA

WAR DIARY
~~INTELLIGENCE SUMMARY.~~

(Erase heading not required.)

Army Form C. 2118.

Instructions regarding War Diaries and Intelligence Summaries are contained in F. S. Regs., Part II. and the Staff Manual respectively. Title pages will be prepared in manuscript.

Hour, Date, Place	Summary of Events and Information	Remarks and references to Appendices
In the field 29.8.16.	Wet day. Completion of reorganization scheme. Flank gun of "A" battery was relieved by A/232. "remaining of the" [crossed out] Right section of "B" battery was relieved by A/231 Remaining detachments of "C" battery were relieved by A/231 and C/230 A.233 Battery was taken over 230th Brigade B 233 — — — — 231st — C 233 Right Section — — — 231st — C 233 Left — — — — 230th — The officers of A & B batteries accompanied their respective batteries CAPT. PEARMAN-SMITH joined 232nd Brigade R.F.A " G.D. WILSON " 231 " (as Adjutant) LIEUT P. ADSHEAD " 232 " A.F. DUFTON " 231 " (as Orderly Officer) " P.B. DUMBELL " 231	PH

Army Form C. 2118.

WAR DIARY
INTELLIGENCE SUMMARY.
(Erase heading not required.)

Instructions regarding War Diaries and Intelligence Summaries are contained in F. S. Regs., Part II. and the Staff Manual respectively. Title pages will be prepared in manuscript.

Hour, Date, Place	Summary of Events and Information	Remarks and references to Appendices
In the field 29.8.16 (continued)	2/LT. W. KEYS. joined 231st Brigade R.F.A. 2/LT. H.A.I. COLLINS joined 231 Brigade R.F.A. 11591 R.S.M. WILLIAMS attached to 232nd R.F.A. 2078 B.S.M. CLARKE joined 231st Brigade R.F.A. all the Headquarted Staff joined the 252nd Brigade R.F.A. Headquarters with the following exceptions. 850 CORP. F. HUNT posted to 46th Div. Arty H.Q. LIEUT-COLONEL. L.G. GISBORNE. C.M.G. took over command of the 232nd Brigade. R.F.A.	[signature] Lieut-Col.

[signature]
Lieut-Col. R.F.A.
Comdg. 263rd Brigade, R.F.A.

WAR   DIARY.

28th: / 29th: August.

Re-organization of Divisional Artillery.

-:-:-:-:-:-:-:-:-:-:-:-:-:-:-:-:-:-

Under instructions from 46th: Divisional Artillery, the 233rd: Brigade R.F.A., was abolished.

The Headquarters were transferred to the 232nd Brigade; A/233 was broken up, the Right Section going to A/230 Battery, the Left Section to B/230 Battery; B/233 was broken up, the Right Section going to B/231., the Left Section to C/231 Battery; C/233 was broken up, the Right Section going to A/231 Battery; the Left Section to C/230 Battery.

The Officers of the 233rd: Brigade were disposed of as follows :-

Lieut. Col. L.G.GISBORNE.C.M.G., posted to Command 232nd Brigade.
R.F.A.

Lieut. F.M.JOYCE., posted to 232nd Brigade.R.F.A.
Lieut. A.F.DUFTON., "   " 232nd   "   """

All Officers of A/233 posted to 230th: Brigade.
All Officers of B/233   "   " 231st: "

Capt. W.S.PEARMAN-SMITH posted to 232nd: Brigade.
Lieut. P.W.ADSHEAD   "   " 231st: "
Capt. W.D.WILSON   "   " 232nd: "

Lieut. P.B.DUMBELL   )
2/Lieut. H.W.KEYS.   )
2/Lieut. H.S.FOSTER.   ) Posted to 231st: Brigade.
2/Lieut.   COLLINS.   )

Lieut. Colonel.

5.9.16.   Commanding 233rd: Brigade R.F.A.

www.ingramcontent.com/pod-product-compliance
Lightning Source LLC
Chambersburg PA
CBHW080855230426

43662CB00013B/2113